DOMESTIC

VIEWS

DOMESTIC

VIEWS

HISTORIC PROPERTIES OWNED OR SUPPORTED BY THE NATIONAL SOCIETY
OF THE COLONIAL DAMES OF AMERICA

PHOTOGRAPHS BY ERIK KVALSVIK

TEXT BY WILLIAM SEALE

THE AMERICAN INSTITUTE OF ARCHITECTS PRESS
WASHINGTON, D.C.

FOR JEAN WARNER EPPERSON

First published in the United States in 1992 by
The American Institute of Architects Press
1735 New York Avenue, N.W.
Washington, D.C. 20006

MAR 9 5

Designed by David Ashton and Company, Ltd., Baltimore, Maryland
Printed by D.W. Friesen, Manitoba, through Four Colour Imports, Ltd.

Photo Credits: page vii, Dumbarton House,
Washington, D.C.; page x, Haywood Hall,
Raleigh, North Carolina; page 294, Fourth
House, Winston-Salem, North Carolina

Library of Congress Cataloging-in-Publication Data

Seale, William.
     Domestic views ; historic properties owned and supported by the
National Society of the Colonial Dames of America / photographs by
Erik Kvalsvik ; text by William Seale.
          p.   cm.
     ISBN 1-55835-079-9 :
     1. Historic buildings—United States.   2. United States—History,
Local.   I. Kvalsvik, Erik.   II. National Society of the Colonial
Dames of America.   III. Title.
E159.S47   1992
973—dc20
                                        92-23510
                                           CIP

CONTENTS

ACKNOWLEDGMENTS

Since The National Society of The Colonial Dames of America undertook this book in 1983, nearly two hundred members of the society have contributed their efforts to the project. It has had the support of national presidents Mildred South Tunnell, Inez Montgomery Bridgeford, and Jean Hyde Watkins. As chairman of the National Commemorative Book Committee, Jean Warner Epperson solicited and organized research materials. Virginia Gurley Meynard assisted with research and reviewed the manuscript. Alice Hunt Daily coordinated marketing. The NSCDA's forty-four state societies provided and helped verify information about the properties, and Isabell Morrison, National Archivist, also contributed research.

We wish to thank all the members of the NSCDA who provided support and hospitality while this book was in preparation. The professional and volunteer staffs of the properties were likewise generous with assistance and information, particularly Don Bergmann, David Floyd, Robert Guffin, Norma K. Lockwood, Lynda Mattingly, Laura Fecych Sprague, and Anne Wallace.

David Ashton's design concept helped shape the book visually, and Cynthia Ware's editing shaped its content. A. Robert Cole helped with photographing the Ximenez-Fatio House and made title suggestions. The end result reflects the publishing expertise of the AIA Press, represented by John Ray Hoke, Jr., publisher; Janet Rumbarger, production manager; and Pamela James Blumgart, editorial assistant.

We also thank Carl A. Ruthstrom for help with preparing the manuscript and Niamh McQuillan for assistance with photography and organization of photographic materials.

Erik Kvalsvik
William Seale

If the history of Europe lives in the great churches and palaces of its past, American history finds continuing expression in old houses. This book is about a particular group of American houses and historic sites from nearly all periods and in well more than half of the states. They are preserved houses open to the public as history museums. Some are grand and were mansions when built, but as many are plain houses built for comfortable shelter long ago, when standards of convenience were different from today's.

This book offers two important opportunities. In the first place, it presents this large group of historic houses through the eye of one photographer. All of the images here were taken by Erik Kvalsvik between 1989 and 1992. Second, bringing the houses together in this way provides a mirror of life in various regions of the United States at various times in history, from the Spanish era in the West to twentieth-century New York. The buildings are grouped regionally and, within regions, chronologically, as strictly as possible, to emphasize their clearest reflections of the American historical landscape.

The historic house museum began in the United States most notably with Mount Vernon in the decade before the Civil War. While Mount Vernon was not the first American house to draw public curiosity, it was certainly the main one, for even in George Washington's lifetime the public went to call, and after his death the pressure of tourism there was constant. By the 1830s a special boat took visitors from the capital to see Washington's home and tomb. The heirs moved out, for privacy's sake, then sold the property for use as a shrine.

The historic house museum as we know it today is the outgrowth of several strains. One, exemplified by Mount Vernon, is the shrine. Another is the broad interest in historic houses and antiques that emerged in the Victorian decades. By the time of the Civil War, writers of fiction had long mined the possibilities in historic houses. James Fenimore Cooper's old halls and roaring fireplaces captured the flavor of a vanished or vanishing pioneer New York, while John Pendleton Kennedy's *Swallow Barn* dealt with an old southern family and its crumbling mansion. No less attracted to the romance of old houses was Nathaniel Hawthorne, whose *House of the Seven Gables*, set in the Salem, Massachusetts of his time, evoked witch trials, guilt, and ancient curses from Puritan New England. William Thackeray gave colonial Virginia a cavalier image in *The Virginians*.

This interest could hardly be called a preservation movement such as we have known for the last thirty years. Bostonians were outraged by the demolition of John Hancock's house during the Civil War, but in the 1880s they nearly permitted the razing of the Bulfinch statehouse, an effort halted by powerful opposition from the rest of the state. The Victorian interest in old houses was in part a fashion and in part nostalgia of the sort that often follows major change in life, in this case that in the wake of the Civil War. Magazine artists sketched sagging houses in remote New England towns, the narrow streets of St. Augustine in Florida, and the towering iron galleries of the French Quarter in New Orleans. To careful renderings of actual parlors and hallways known to early Americans they added costumed figures, recreating old times.

On an everyday level, popular taste was invaded in the early 1870s by the Queen Anne style, inspired by the English cottage, the cozy vernacular dwelling of pre-Georgian times—"the days of good Queen Anne." Exposed timber framing, color-washed plaster, bare floors, quaintly shaped windows, and flat, round-edged roof tiles were a few of the elements brought into this architectural mode and mixed freely in the manner of a house built by an ordinary country carpenter. Not long after the Queen Anne made its American sweep designers began to substitute architectural detailing perceived as "colonial" for imported English motifs. The most obvious expressions of this were wood shingles, replacing English tiles, and wooden "gingerbread," which already had some tradition in American cottage building.

In the tasteful interior of the time, one's personality was to show through in special arrangements and in the selection of objects. Antiques made their appearance. Furniture manufacturers realized fine profits from producing spinning wheels as decorative accents for colonial parlors, and spinning wheels also appeared reconfigured as chairs and tables. Old teapots, silver spoons, pretty fans, and collections of dishes, books, and other antiquities from times just beyond modern memory gave the Queen Anne interiors their contrived character.

The next generation abandoned most of this, but not the motifs. Already by the end of the 1880s a general interest had appeared in more believable renditions of historic architecture in new buildings. In architecture this new historicity is labeled Beaux-Arts, after the teachings of the Ecole des Beaux-Arts in Paris, which left their mark on many European city centers at the time. In the United States this era gave us many of our columned state capitols, great post offices, and other public buildings. On the domestic scene it spawned a revival of American historical architectural styles. Architects and builders sought out historic houses for inspiration, some of them among the houses in this book. At its beginning the Colonial Revival was dominated by New England historical design features because the leading residential architects, based mostly in New York, found their sources nearby. Time saw this expand, particularly in the twentieth century. California's Spanish Mission Revival, a variation on the Colonial Revival, was well underway by 1900. Often the revivals were inspired by literature, which gave them romantic definition.

Concurrent with the historical revivals was the restoration movement, which was strongest in New England but was not unknown elsewhere. In Virginia, for example, outsiders, in many cases from New York, bought up eighteenth-century plantation houses in substantial numbers and restored them, while also giving them a "period" look reflecting styles current in Edwardian England, not the past of Virginia. This image lingers even today in Virginia's historic house museums. But restoration was often more a case of remodeling, of adapting buildings to sharp images of romantic history that were likely to be in conflict with the original appearance of the building. An example of this was the restoration of the 1610 Palace of the Governors at Santa Fe, which in 1913 gained a "Spanish" look of a sort it had never had and still retains.

A third line in the genealogy of the house museum is the development of a style of architecture and decorating that held great appeal because it seemed appropriate to the United States. This strain became emotional after World War I, when the radical change in the world and the flood of eastern Europeans to American shores questioned the traditional security of Anglo-Saxon domination. The reaction to this on one level was the glorification of American antiques and their incorporation into appealing domestic settings which were monuments to a history that seemed to represent a better America.

Efforts in this period to recreate the past accompanied a profound sense not only of change, but indeed of loss. Older cultures have naturally preceded the United States in this interest, for until this century this country looked largely forward. George Washington would be pleased but surely puzzled by the museum use of his lanky wooden home; odder still to his view would be America's preservation as a structure of Sulgrave Manor in Northamptonshire, England, which was his ancestral home—a fact of which he was unaware. "I have not the least Solicitude to trace our Ancestry," he once wrote to a nephew.

Organizations of various kinds became involved in creating these monuments. The National Society of The Colonial Dames of America was one of many patriotic organizations that took up the trend of the period room and the historic house museum, although it would be the accumulation of properties over many more years that would constitute the society's more important work. Perhaps the greatest landmark of the post–World War I antiquarian movement was the American Wing at the Metropolitan Museum of Art in New York, opened in 1924. "We are honoring our fathers and our mothers, our grandfathers and our grandmothers, that their art may live long in the land which the Lord hath given us," stated the museum's chairman, Robert W. de Forest, at the dedication ceremony. "For the first time an American museum is giving a prominent place to American domestic art and exhibiting it in such a way as to show its historical development."

The American Wing made a profound impression on American taste in the interiors of houses. It was followed a mere five years later by the commencement of the restoration of Williamsburg, a major event in American architecture that unfolded over many years, its mark ever deeper in America's view of its past. Trying to explore adequately Williamsburg's influences in this area would be difficult indeed. For all its honesty, Williamsburg was as much a shrine as the earlier romantic restorations, but it projected an image that was adapted and adopted all over the United States in many different, and usually opposing, contexts. The influence was all the more significant because Williamsburg was born anew against the background of the Depression, almost in defiance of impending disaster. And depression was followed by world war.

There was little change in the idea of the historic house from the early 1930s until the late 1960s. Vast information was assembled through the Historic American Buildings Survey and the Index of Design, federally funded programs that were outgrowths of the Depression recovery plan. Significantly, this material was national in scope, and even today it is remarkable to review the production of that period and imagine its extent, its opening of new trails into territory where no one had gone before for that purpose. Meanwhile the number of historic house museums increased into the many thousands, some state and national sites, some owned by private groups, from local historical societies to nationwide organizations like the Colonial Dames. By and large, the museums were reflections in one way or another of Williamsburg, at the most historical, or of the older, romantic view of history.

The 1960s and particularly the 1970s saw the first major visible changes in historic house museums as the nation approached the bicentennial of the American Revolution. Under the direction of the National Park Service, the restoration of Independence Hall in Philadelphia introduced and indeed in some cases invented technical fields in historic restoration. The sorts of information produced by this project—for example, through paint color research—brought truth to the restoration process that had not been there before. An era becoming possessed by technology responded quickly to the use of technology in historic restoration. It provided a kind of justification, long needed, in its promise of sometimes elusive documentary accuracy.

The impact of this new approach was evident in the work of historians as well. Documentary investigation of historic buildings took on a wholly new character, moving from the mere search for facts about furniture or additions to buildings into questions about personalities and ways of life that would influence the contents and arrangements of the houses and inspire more accurate interpretation. Many of the houses in this book reflect in various degrees this altered approach to the historic house. This publication falls in time well into the movement, yet also at its beginnings, for the concept expands yearly, as does the educational importance of the house museum.

The National Society of The Colonial Dames of America was founded in 1891 as a patriotic organization to engage in educational and commemorative works. Membership qualifications are based on a woman's documented descent from citizens of British America, and who the citizen was may make a difference. Unlike the Daughters of the American Revolution, with which it is sometimes confused, the organization has the specific directive to avoid politics. With the exception of politics as it applies to historic preserva-

tion, the Dames have remained steady on this course. While by its charter the organization can own historic property, it was not the original purpose of the Colonial Dames to enter the house museum business. Yet today the various state chapters of the Colonial Dames own or are otherwise affiliated with eighty-seven historic sites of one kind or another, most of them houses. (A complete checklist appears following the text.)

The story of the Dames' houses follows that of the historic house museum. It will be clear from the photographs that the houses run the gamut of attitudes toward how historic houses should be, from the 1930s, when the buildings were kept as monuments and shrines, until the present day, when they are seen as history museums. The direction currently is toward the latter, and has been since the Bicentennial. As houses have come to be museums, the focus of their preservation has changed from decorative arts and beautiful things to human habitation and historical context. Usually this shift has called for a different viewpoint on the property.

An example is the Ximenez-Fatio House, a late eighteenth-century house in St. Augustine, Florida. When the museum was established in the early 1930s, the Spanish-style Fatio House was interpreted as an inn, for which purpose it was actually built in the 1790s. Research in recent years revealed a more flexible and vital history of a succession of women who used the rambling building in the nineteenth century as a winter hotel. Conversion to this story involved the virtual refurnishing of the house to represent the span of time from the Seminole War in the 1820s to the 1870s. The change presented an opportunity for an interpetation that drew on women's history, but also on that of enslaved Africans, the Majorcan community, and the dawning hotel industry in Florida. The "realistic" approach to the furnishing of the rooms, based on careful research, brings forth a vivid and compelling image of that time in St. Augustine, in contrast to the earlier Spanish period interpretation of the restored downtown.

Many of the houses pictured here represent the same approach to reinterpretation, and this has been of particular interest in Erik Kvalsvik's photography. He has captured the tremendous variety of texture and effect that is achieved in the new sort of interiors, which are not coordinated according to tastes in decorative arts or interior design—the natural direction of the shrine houses—but by probable patterns of actual use at a time in the past. All houses are not, of course, suited to the strictly historical approach. An example is the Colonial Dames Museum House, the New York headquarters building in Manhattan, where superb interiors by the architect Richard Henry Dana, Jr., express Colonial Revival sensibilities of the 1930s, so strongly inspired by the American Wing.

All the houses in this book reflect the work of volunteers, most of whom would qualify, at least at the outset of their efforts, as amateurs. In some cases preservation was the issue, and a house was rescued from demolition, by relocation, as with Kent Plantation House in Louisiana, or by reconstruction using original materials, as with Wilton in Virginia, or by a restoration on site, as with the Silas Deane House in Connecticut. Professional assistance was nearly always involved, initially in the participation of an architect. Increasingly in recent years the architect has become one in a team of specialists. The houses have proven themselves to be historic documents, to be read and reread, questioned and requestioned, yielding new information as the scholar's ability and the technology of restoration improve. In turn, as the historic house genre comes to accept this historical process, existing museum houses are inevitably re-restored, an effort seen the most dramatically at Gunston Hall in Virginia.

This book exists neither to extol nor to explain, but to present the houses for the enjoyment of their authenticity or beauty—or on any level one's visual curiosity may reach. They represent many years of hard work and millions of volunteer dollars. The contents of the rooms show some decades of antique-searching. Most of what you see here has virtually vanished from the everyday market of old furnishings, and the stories of how these objects were acquired for the

different houses are legion. Looking through the pictures it is not hard to imagine the challenge and the pleasure the search provided.

The objects fall into three categories: the original documented piece from that particular place; the generic piece that research has shown to be appropriate to that place; and, last, the reproduction, into which area fall most of the floor coverings, curtains, wallpapers, and the like—things that deteriorated or became obsolete and were thrown out. Recreations never quite match the originals, so the early wallpaper in the Joseph Webb House in Wethersfield, Connecticut, and the brickwork kitchen stove, rebuilt on the original foundations in the Hermann-Grima House in New Orleans, are particular treasures. No more, however, than the remarkable early twentieth-century bathroom in the Overholser Mansion in Oklahoma City.

What do these historic places represent in total? The answer is a cross-section. They are not all architectural masterpieces, but some are; their furnishings are not always the finest specimens, although some are. Each of the places represents a region's idea of an embodiment of its history, so they are local expressions both as historical artifacts and as contemporary symbols. National trends in museums and historical inquiry naturally reflect in them, and sometimes they are understandably out of date in this area; but they are often in step with the times, and in a few cases quite ahead. They are adapted from their original uses and revised as museums for educational purposes, all of them ongoing in their public service. Together they are a compelling sampling— a family album—of the pasts of us all.

THE OLD SOUTH

The surviving buildings of the Old South, where English culture was first permanently introduced to what we now call the United States, are evidence of lives that seemed to cling to English custom, yet were the first to embrace democratic ideals. The second loyalty did not decry aristocratic images in architecture and flourished paradoxically along with slavery. The houses here range in date from the 1714 Hanover House in Clemson, South Carolina, to West Virginia's Craik-Patton House of 1834. English taste is mirrored in Richmond's Wilton, while the Burgwin-Wright House in Wilmington, North Carolina, shows the beginnings of American ways of building, a development complete in Raleigh's Haywood Hall and Rosedale in Charlotte.

HANOVER HOUSE 1714

Clemson, South Carolina

This frame house stood originally at the headwaters of the west branch of the Cooper River, on a 1,000-acre plantation inherited by the builder from his father. Paul de St. Julien was the third generation of his family to live in the colony of South Carolina, the immigrant being his grandfather, Pierre de St. Julien, a Huguenot who ended his family's wanderings—from France, at least—by settling in America in the seventeenth century. Paul married his first cousin Marie Aimée Ravenel and moved to the plantation in 1714.

His new house was framed in oak and sided and roofed in cypress, and the principal rooms were paneled in walnut. On one of the chimneys St. Julien inscribed *peu à peu*, the motto of the house, from the saying, "Little by little the bird builds its nest." The house is not large, but it looks tall, with the second floor concealed beneath a gambrel roof pierced by dormer windows. There are four rooms to a floor, each with a fireplace. Kitchen and storerooms are in the basement, with the living and bedrooms on the floors above.

Hanover House—named later by an in-law for the Georgian kings—remained in the same family until the 1930s, when it was threatened by the building of a dam for a hydroelectric plant. The architectural historian Thomas T. Waterman proclaimed Hanover House unique among survivors from colonial America and called for its preservation. In 1940 the house was moved to the campus of Clemson University, a journey of over 200 miles inland from the coast. Twenty-two years later it was restored and opened to the public.

WILTON HOUSE MUSEUM
1753, 1934

Richmond, Virginia

Wilton, built as the home of William Randolph III, was one of Virginia's finest eighteenth-century Georgian houses. The Wilton of today is a 1930s reconstruction from original materials on a new site that, like the old, is adjacent to the James River. Wilton is justifiably celebrated for its fully paneled interiors, but the exterior, understated in the Georgian way, has quite as much to recommend it. The heavy brick walls, laid up in Flemish bond, are relieved at the windows by rubbed work, that is, preparation of the bricks for laying by rubbing them together so that they fit tightly with little mortar around the wooden window structure. Wilton's simplicity of form and materials is a foil for its ornamented doorway; but even the doorway is simple, compared to its counterparts at other houses of this time.

The painted paneling inside, all pine, is simple in its design, mere rectangles, fielded, with restrained ornament in window alcoves and in the chimney reveals beside fireplaces. Like Gunston Hall, it is a house in which fine craftsmanship, unencumbered by anything that could be called frilly, becomes part of the design. Scholars have speculated that Richard Taliaferro of Williamsburg may have built Wilton, but the connection has never been firmly established. Wilton belongs to what can be called a Virginia type, a borrowing from a British mode found in country towns in houses built for the clergy or the gentry. Its furnishings represent colonial and late eighteenth-century craftsmanship, many of the objects of Virginia provenance, including portraits of Randolphs who knew Wilton when it was young.

Lorton, Virginia

Gunston Hall was the home of George Mason, the complex and irascible patriot who wrote the Virginia Bill of Rights and thus influenced all other such statements of human rights, including the French Declaration of the Rights of Man. For his project at Gunston he brought the carver and tradesman William Buckland from England. Buckland was to have a major influence on building in the Chesapeake Bay region.

In a rural Potomac River setting, Gunston Hall is a house of surprises, a mansion within a cottage. Its builders made a stringent effort to keep it looking small, yet its interiors are among the richest known from colonial America. The demanding character of its owner is seen in the tight, sturdy building and its fine materials. That there could be so much house under so seemingly small a roof is a continual fascination of Gunston Hall. Its compactness suggests a close, private family life. Structural research has revealed much about the house in the Masons' time. An interior window in the stairwell, long buried but now opened up, was designed to borrow light for a dark linen room. In the ornate parlor or eating room the bare pine walls, recently stripped of silk damask, show "ghost" marks of an original fireplace surround, inspiring an architect's ornate conjecture, drawn on paper.

When Mason's son sold Gunston Hall in 1833, he noted that its 5,000 acres "abounded with deer and the river with canvas-back ducks and other wild fowls; that the estate had numerous springs of excellent water." Its grounds still have some of the remoteness and special charm that the Masons must have enjoyed.

JOEL LANE HOUSE 1760s

Raleigh, North Carolina

The oldest house in North Carolina's capital, the Joel Lane House is documented as standing four years before the Declaration of Independence but was probably built in the 1760s. It is an architectural form familiar all along the middle and upper Atlantic coast, especially in New England and Virginia. North Carolinians adapted the style in a small way by giving it extra verticality in a heightened main floor and a gambrel roof. In the eighteenth century the house stood on a large, prosperous farm, where Joel Lane lived with his household of twelve children and his twenty-seven slaves. Lane died in 1795, and the house was sold out of his family in 1803. In the simple, well-crafted rooms the first local courts met in colonial times; the North Carolina Committee of Correspondence convened here in 1776. The late eighteenth-century furnishings are enhanced by some excellent North Carolina–made pieces, including several believed to have belonged to Joel Lane.

BURGWIN-WRIGHT HOUSE 1770

Wilmington, North Carolina

John Burgwin was an Englishman who came to America when young as an employee of Hooper, Alexander & Company of Charleston and Wilmington, a mercantile firm with strong connections to England. He stayed on, opening his own company and serving in various high official positions in the circles of the royal governor of North Carolina. At his peak he had five ships and was doing business in London, Barbados, and Amsterdam, as well as along the Atlantic coast. His portrait by John Singleton Copley shows a man with a sharp, penetrating look, quill in hand, ready for business.

In addition to this town house, Burgwin built on one of his plantations a large country house, the Hermitage, where he and his children spent the summers. Loyalist at the outbreak of the Revolution, Burgwin and his family fled to England. When his property was confiscated in 1778, he hurried to New York and, after gaining recognition as a patriot, made his way to North Carolina, where his properties were restored. He sold his town house to Judge Joshua G. Wright in 1799.

The interiors of the Burgwin-Wright House are treated in the eighteenth-century manner. The "great room" upstairs has buffet niches such as those in English dining rooms. Eighteenth- and early nineteenth-century American and English furniture is used in the principal rooms, that in the yellow supper room English, and early North Carolina vernacular furniture is used in the basement service rooms.

HAYWOOD HALL HOUSE AND GARDENS 1798

Raleigh, North Carolina

John Haywood, treasurer of North Carolina for forty years, commenced construction of this house in 1798, and he and his wife Eliza lived here for the rest of their lives, he until 1827 and she until 1832. It remained in the ownership of their descendants until 1977, when it was left with an accumulation of furnishings for use as a museum.

The late Federal house, with its double-stack porches, seems architecturally cohesive without, but its interiors represent a lapse into the colonial vernacular, especially in the ornamental parlor fireplace surround, with heavy columns and cornice, all gaudily marbled, decrying Federal restraint. Often such departures give old American houses their best quality, and here their extravagance imparts a naive charm. Haywood Hall stands, gleaming white, in a fine old garden, where crêpe myrtle, magnolia, pecan, and fig trees dominate, among countless shrubs that date from the family's long occupancy.

ROSEDALE circa 1805

Charlotte, North Carolina

Made of North Carolina pine, with an oak frame, Rosedale is solid; some of its sills are sixty feet long and nearly a foot square. Parts of the structure that have never been exposed to the weather still have the scent of the old trees. The original builder, Archibald Frew, is known to have used French wallpapers in the rooms, for a fragment of one such paper survives. William Davidson acquired Rosedale and its farm in 1819. A state senator and later a United States congressman, Davidson deeded the house in 1833 to his son-in-law, Dr. David T. Caldwell, husband of Davidson's daughter Harriet. Rosedale descended through the Caldwell family until 1986, when it was acquired by purchase as a museum.

Rosedale's building history includes repairs but few real changes. Restoration work that began in 1989 is seen here in process, from the basement kitchen, with its temporary props, to the upper floors, with their old woodwork and mantels. Research on the use of the house in the time of the first Davidson has revealed paint graining and a variety of brilliant paint colors, as well as the character of alterations.

OVAL BALLROOM, HOLLIDAY-CAMERON HOUSE 1830

Fayetteville, North Carolina

This handsome interior, built as a wing to an existing house by John A. Cameron, presents the interesting architectural effect of an oval set inside a semioctagonal projection. The architect was Captain William Nichols, an Englishman who adorned North Carolina with many handsome buildings in the decade or so following the War of 1812. Remodeling architect of the statehouse at Raleigh, Nichols had built plantation houses and public buildings elsewhere in the state, not the least the Gothic town hall and city market in Fayetteville.

The Oval Ballroom, with its Greek Revival detailing, is in fact a bow-ended room, being an elongated half-oval. It is banded by Ionic pilasters and crowned by a deep cornice. The floor, of broad pine boards, was almost certainly covered with canvas that was waxed for dancing, or occasionally decorated with a colorful scene in chalk. In this elegant interior, the walls lined with chairs, the central floor cleared for country dances—waltzes later on—the Fayetteville gentry danced and enjoyed the bounty of the adjacent dining room.

In the 1950s the Holliday-Cameron House was razed, and, lest Fayetteville lose all of this favorite landmark, a group of citizens acquired the ballroom wing and moved it up the street to safe ground. It has been restored and kept as the remarkable interior that it is, open to the public.

CRAIK-PATTON HOUSE 1834

Charleston, West Virginia

The Reverend James Craik, also a lawyer, was the grandson of George Washington's physician in Alexandria, Virginia. By the time he built this house, the movement from the eastern seaboard to new land, in this case to the part of Virginia we know as West Virginia, was a generation old. Reverend Craik occupied the house for a decade and then moved on to Kentucky. By the time of the Civil War it was the home of Confederate Brigadier General George S. Patton, who was killed in the Cedar Creek campaign in the Virginia valley in 1864—the great-grandfather of General George S. Patton.

The house is an airy cottage, of frame construction, set very high on a fine base of cut stone. The portico, with its Tuscan columns, projects from the main block sufficiently to lighten the mass. It might be classified as Greek Revival because of the portico, but the detailing of the house is earlier, in fact Federal, and in a decidedly Virginian vernacular. The unusual plan is dominated by a great central room—a feature one encounters occasionally in southern houses. Its chairs and sofa date from the time when this region was still Virginia. The Craik-Patton House has been moved twice, most recently in 1973, when it was situated in a wooded park overlooking the Kanawha River.

NEW ENGLAND

Settlement in New England began soon after that in the South, and a more nearly complete transplant of life in rural England could not, by 1750, be found. The severe climate and the presence of often-hostile Indians encouraged the development of a colonial civilization based in small towns. A more widespread and localized political authority and England's faraway conflict between Crown and Commonwealth in the seventeenth century helped New England develop a greater economic self-reliance than the South. With the exception of the 1808 Boston residence of the historian William Prescott, all the New England houses here originated in the eighteenth century. No tone of aristocracy masks the vernacular quality of most of these buildings. Built of wood, they are either weathered by exposure or gleam beneath generations of paint, their scale that of the farm and village houses of England.

QUINCY HOMESTEAD 1706, 1904

Quincy, Massachusetts

The Quincy family purchased about 400 acres of land from the British crown in 1635, built on it in 1706 and 1730, and stayed on until the close of the French and Indian War in 1763, when they sold the property. The homestead served as a summer place for the Boston-based Quincys. Over the years, into the early twentieth century, they developed the house into a tall, striking mansion of frame, with a steep roof and bold fenestration, including heroic dormer windows. A number of architectural changes have left it with a strong New England Federal character on the exterior and an interior that is consciously "colonial," reflecting the early twentieth-century Colonial Revival, here interpreted by the masterly hand of Joseph E. Chandler, a leading proponent of the style.

Quincy Homestead is furnished with New England antiques, largely from the eighteenth and early nineteenth centuries, including high-post beds, Windsor chairs, monumental knife boxes, and a fine Franklin fireplace or stove. The house is set in a deep garden with great shade trees, a variety of fruit trees, vines, lilacs, day lilies, roses, and herbs, all laid out authentically as a pleasure garden of the mid-eighteenth century. An outbuilding contains a combination carriage and sleigh that belonged to John Hancock of Boston.

GOVERNOR STEPHEN HOPKINS HOUSE 1707, 1742

Providence, Rhode Island

Stephen Hopkins was born in Providence, the descendant of original settlers who had come from England with Rhode Island's founder, Roger Williams. Self-educated and a surveyor by occupation, Hopkins became involved in public life at an early age. By his mid-thirties he was a leading political figure in the colony, and he and his family became rich from the shipping business. Hopkins and his wife Sarah lived on a farm until 1742, when the pressure of affairs brought them back to Providence. They bought land with a small house on it, soon increasing the house to its present size.

Stephen and Sarah Hopkins filled the house with seven children and busy lives.

From its small, low-ceilinged rooms Stephen conducted business and politics. When Sarah died after twenty-seven years of marriage, he remarried. In politics his was a dynasty, for he was elected to ten successive one-year terms as governor and moved between the alternate capitals of Providence and Newport. He counted Benjamin Franklin among his friends, and George Washington visited his house twice.

The small, red-painted New England house is in a remarkable state of preservation, even though it has been moved twice, in 1804 and again in 1927, when the entrance was relocated to accommodate the new site. The whitewashed plaster and paint-grained woodwork recreate the mid-eighteenth-century decor.

MARTIN HOUSE 1728

North Swansea, Massachusetts

Established in 1728 by John Martin, a first-generation New Englander whose father and grandfather had immigrated from Somersetshire to join relatives in Massachusetts, the Martin farm remained in the same family for 207 years before becoming a museum property. The men of the family in early days were surveyors, which was a lucrative way to make a living as well as a way to acquire land. The wood-shingled farmhouse which John Martin and his wife Mary occupied is a characteristic New England type, in which the rooms of the timber-frame structure nestle around a great central chimney and are made tight from the fierce winters by plastered walls and fielded wood paneling. It is a good house, sturdily built, and forthright in its expression of a strong regional vernacular.

The interior is restored to the eighteenth-century period of the Martins' ownership. John Martin's musket and powderhorn hang over his mantelpiece, surveying an English drop-leaf table and Windsor chairs of the kind imported to America in his time. The family portraits hang on old plaster walls framed by resurrected eighteenth-century paint colors, the blues and greens composed of lead white and pigment mixed on the site, then painted on and varnished over, sharing the simple decor with lime whitewash that was probably renewed annually. The farm itself is gone, but the Martin House, in its ample green glade, survives as a reminder of what one Martin more than a century ago called his "honest yeomen" ancestors.

WHITEHALL HOUSE MUSEUM 1729

Middletown, Rhode Island

The Irish-born philospher and divine, George Berkeley, dean of Londonderry, came to America in 1729 to found a college in Bermuda to train colonists and American Indians for the clergy. While he waited for funding from England he made Newport his base, acquired a 96-acre farm, and built Whitehall onto an existing small house. In his household were his young wife, the portrait painter John Smibert, and a large company of his intellectural followers. Berkeley was determined to represent his mission appropriately, and the house for its time was pretentious. The pedimented entrance door, with its Ionic pilasters, anticipates an architectural sophistication yet to appear in Newport and stands out with a certain splendor against the red-painted clapboards of the exterior and the more predictable New England form of the building.

The attempt to establish a college was unsuccessful. Berkeley gave up after three years and returned to London, but not before he had had great influence on education in America, in part through involvement in the founding of Columbia and Brown universities. Berkeley, eventually bishop of Cloyne, never forgot America. He sent hundreds of books to Yale College, to which he also gave Whitehall. Yale held onto the property for some 150 years. Its fortunes were various. During the Revolution the British occupied it; kept at times as a tavern, at times as a hotel, it declined over the years. About a hundred years ago it was rescued by a group of Newport citizens, who opened it to the public.

WEBB HOUSE
At a conference held at Webb House,
Wethersfield May 22 1781, General Washington,
and the Count de Rochambeau made final
plans for the joint action of the American
and French armies which resulted in the
Battle of Yorktown and the surrender of
Cornwallis.

Headquarters of the National Society of Colonial
Dames of America in the State of Connecticut

JOSEPH WEBB HOUSE 1752

Wethersfield, Connecticut

Like a number of other houses in this book, this one had no architect; but its proportions and details show the influence of English pattern books. Judah Wright of Farmington framed the roof and connected the new house to an earlier one, which was left as an ell in the new composition. When she remarried in 1763, after Joseph Webb's death, Mehitabel Webb gave the house to her son Joseph, who made it his home. So elaborate was his entertaining that his house was nicknamed "Hospitality Hall." It was quarters for George Washington for five days in May 1781. In the parlor he met with the comte de Rochambeau to plan the rendezvous of American and French forces at Yorktown, where the Revolution was won. Fame has renamed Webb's parlor the "council room."

Through a long succession of owners the house remained relatively unchanged, until early in this century, when, paradoxically, the well-known collector and antiques scholar Wallace Nutting made alterations considered damaging by today's standards of authenticity, including the addition of wood paneling and murals. Public life began for the Joseph Webb House when it was opened as a tea room. Restoration based on scholarship began under nonprofit ownership in the 1920s, and the interiors reflect research conducted since then. The colors of the decor are those used in the house in the eighteenth century. In the bedroom where Washington slept, the large-pattern feathered wallpaper that greeted him is crowned with its original glittery border on which mica has been scattered in paste.

TATE HOUSE 1755

Portland, Maine

This indomitable house, the clapboards of which have never known paint, has survived Portland's sometimes stormy history to prevail as its most important colonial monument. It stands with its back to the freshwater Stroudwater River, which once ran gristmills and sawmills; in front is the brackish Fore River, once the site of warehouses and stores that accompanied the Tates' prosperous business in ships' masts, cut from the Maine forests. The Tate House is a New England house, centered on a great chimney, but it is more, embellished with a splendid front door crowned by a fanlight and pediment and flanking pilasters. Most interesting in the architectural composition are the horizontals formed by the windows, including on the roof a setback penthouse level with windows all across.

Captain George Tate, who built the house in 1755, came to America with his wife Mary and his family as the agent for the English company that held a monopoly on providing masts for the royal navy. White pine trees seventy feet tall and twenty-four inches and larger in diameter were reserved for this purpose. The restriction on lumbering became the principal political issue among the Maine colonists at the time of the Revolution, and the Tates' business, central to the controversy, never recovered after the business of supplying ships' masts entered the private sector under the new republic. George Tate and his sons eventually fell into bankruptcy. Although the house has not been restored to its earliest period, that colorful past is represented in the museum interiors, refurnished with eighteenth- and early nineteenth-century objects.

MOFFATT-LADD HOUSE 1763

Portsmouth, New Hampshire

This elegant colonial house occupies a rise of land above the deep, rapid tidal waters of the Piscataqua River at Portsmouth Harbor. Built in 1763, it remained in the hands of Moffatt descendants until just before World War I. Captain John Moffatt came to America while in his twenties and married Catherine Cutt, of a prominent New Hampshire political family, and settled in the colonies. The Moffatts built the Portsmouth house as a wedding present for their son Samuel. When the extravagant Samuel fled to England to avoid debtor's prison, the elder Moffatts took the house for themselves. Here they lived through the American Revolution. In the third generation the house came under the Ladd name by the marriage of the Moffatts' granddaughter to Alexander Ladd.

The three-story, hip-roofed, clapboard house is the first of a type later familiar in Portsmouth. Quoins, hooded windows, and other late Georgian architectural embellishments stand out against the dark-painted wooden walls. The interior's elegant finish climaxes in the richly executed staircase, one of colonial America's finest, all the more dramatic in the context of the simpler rooms, with their painted floors. The careful furnishing is the result of years of historical research. Portraits of the Moffatts and Ladds hang on the walls, and fine eighteenth-century New England and English furnishings re-create their setting. Upholsteries, slip-covers, and hangings are carefully copied from early examples, and the yellow wall-paper in the captain's bedroom is repro-duced from a fragment found in the house still bearing the tax stamp of George III.

SILAS DEANE HOUSE 1766

Wethersfield, Connecticut

One of Mehitabel Webb's callers at the Joseph Webb house (see pages 64-71) was Silas Deane, the lawyer who helped the elder Joseph Webb's widow settle her husband's estate. She grew to depend on him, and after a two-year courtship they were married and moved subsequently to this frame house with paneled rooms and a notable two-story stairhall that occupies a corner of the front. One son, Jesse, was born to them there, and Mehitabel Deane died. Silas Deane then married Elizabeth Saltonstall, whose high political connections in New England encouraged his ambitions for public service.

George Washington, en route to Boston to take command of the Continental army, dined with the Deanes here in 1775.

By then the Wethersfield attorney was deeply involved in the affairs of the Revolution. In 1775 he was sent to France secretly to try to enlist the aid of Louis XVI. Eventually a steady stream of arms and ammunition began to cross the sea. During the Revolution Deane remained in France, in unhappy rivalry with his subsequent colleagues in his mission, Benjamin Franklin and Arthur Lee. In 1789, broken in health, his fortune gone, his wife dead, he prepared to return home, and died before his ship sailed. His house is his principal memorial, its interiors restored with New England Chippendale and Queen Anne Chinese-type seating pieces and eighteenth-century prints and pewter to give an impression of what it must have been like when Deane lived here.

ISAAC STEVENS HOUSE 1788

Wethersfield, Connecticut

Slumbering behind its rusty picket fence, the Isaac Stevens House seems very American in its simple rectangular outline and its setting of shade trees. It was built in the 1780s during the Confederation, and its style recalls the Georgian vernacular, although the facade anticipates a very ordinary sort of American house of the first half of the nineteenth century. Among his other business endeavors, Isaac Stevens operated a livery stable on this site. He dealt in cash, unlike the farmers and many of the merchants of the region, and he seems to have had the money to keep a substantial house. Although nothing is known of the original contents, the interior was executed with some thought, as evidenced by the woodwork and by window shutters that slide in tracks to completely cover the windows. Broad pine floor boards, probably covered originally except in the summer, have been revived and waxed. The house has seen many changes over time, but research has revealed the original paint colors, and restoration has introduced furnishings of many types from the first years of the United States.

WILLIAM HICKLING PRESCOTT HOUSE 1808

Boston, Massachusetts

The architect of this house on Boston's Beacon Hill was Asher Benjamin, one of the best-known architects and builders of the early republic. His reputation was based more on his widely circulated "how-to" books than on his buildings. His 1806 *American Builder's Companion* and subsequent handbooks probably provided models for houses, churches, and courthouses as far as the Pacific coast. This house, at 55 Beacon Street, was built for James Colburn, a self-made businessman and a widower who remarried to Sarah Prince soon after moving in in 1808. But the most famous occupant at this address was the historian William H. Prescott, who enlarged the house to hold his valuable library. Here Prescott, already famous for his poetic *History of the Conquest of Mexico*, completed *History of the Conquest of Peru* and began *History of the Reign of Philip II*. He lived and worked in the house until his death in 1859.

A youthful free-for-all in college had left Prescott partially blind. He added large glass panes to the windows of his sunny study to have the maximum light to work by. An 1850s woodcut of the upstairs study shows his bookcases—pictured here—screened with roller window shades to protect the bindings from the sun. William Makepeace Thackeray visited him here in 1852 and in conversation got the idea for *The Virginians*. The study is about as it looked when Prescott used it every day and the leading literary figures of the day came to call. Downstairs, the house is furnished to represent the Boston of the time when it was built.

THE MID·ATLANTIC

Settlement came to this region in the later seventeenth century. As the architecture developed, its character was varied by strong Old World influences, not only English, but also Dutch in New York and German in Pennsylvania and Delaware. Dutch New York was taken by the English in 1664 and presented to the king's brother, the duke of York. New Jersey, Pennsylvania, Delaware, and Maryland were likewise proprietor- ships, with extensive systems of land rents and fees that continued in some cases even beyond the Revolution. The architecture reflects these aristocratic origins in a formal Georgian tradition in such houses as Stenton in Germantown outside Philadelphia and Mount Clare in Baltimore. In the capital, Washington, style was united in the neoclassical believed universally appropriate to a republic.

STENTON 1723

Philadelphia, Pennsylvania

James Logan, Stenton's original owner, came to Pennsylvania in 1699 as secretary to William Penn. Two years later Penn returned to England and gave Logan the enviable opportunity of remaining as his lawyer in charge of the business of the proprietors of the colony. With this entrée, Logan rose in the colonial government, becoming chief justice at the age of fifty-seven and governor thereafter. While he was still in his forties, he and his wife Sarah built Stenton, a country house in fashionable Germantown, outside Philadelphia.

In the Logans' time Stenton was a farm, and vegetable and flower gardens grew even beyond the brick walls that surrounded the house. Logan, an amateur astronomer, had an observatory on the roof; he had a library of 3,000 volumes and possessed a reading knowledge of seven ancient and modern languages. After his death his son lived on at Stenton and acquired much of its best furniture. During the American Revolution the house was headquarters for one day in 1777 of General Washington and later of British General Sir William Howe, who used the mansion as a place from which to direct operations in the Battle of Germantown.

Stenton continued in the Logan family until 1900, and since then it has been operated as a house museum. The house contains many pieces of Logan family furniture along with others made in well-known Philadelphia workshops. One of the beds, covered in check, and a bed tray were made by Thomas Tufft in the 1770s or 1780s and may have been Logan pieces. Stenton retains many of its outbuildings, and the gardens, restored some seventy-five years ago, are extensive.

PEACHFIELD PLANTATION HOUSE 1725, 1931

Mount Holly, New Jersey

Henry Burr built the central part of Peachfield in 1725, and when his son John added the west wing seven years later, he set his initals and those of his wife, Keziah, into one of the new walls. This house remained in the Burr family until 1896, 182 years after the original purchase of the land in 1714. It is a rambling stone house of a characteristic Delaware Valley type with interiors both plastered and paneled in wood. With the exception of the front wall, the house is a reconstruction for private residential use of the original struc-ture, which was destroyed by lightning and an ensuing fire in 1928. The house rose again in 1931 with the addition of some new paneling and other elements, all under the direction of Grognard Oakie, a well known Colonial Revival architect. Recreated as an architectural specimen, it represents an approach of that time to restoration, endorsed nationally in the restoration of Williamsburg beginning in the early thirties. As a house museum, Peachfield is identified as a reproduction and is furnished to reflect the eras of the Burrs, principally the eighteenth-century generations, but later ones as well.

VAN CORTLANDT HOUSE MUSEUM 1748

The Bronx, New York

This three-story fieldstone mansion was built on lands that had once been hunting grounds of the Mohican Indians and are now part of Van Cortlandt Park in the Bronx. It is a very early house museum, first opened in 1896. The residence of Frederick Van Cortlandt, son of a rich Manhattan merchant and mayor of New York, the estate was one of the region's finest during the revolutionary years, when George Washington stayed there. Other military leaders, British as well as Americans, used the house. The building was restored in 1913-1917 under the direction of the architect Norman Isham, who made many authentic alterations but added extensive fielded paneling in the halls and staircases for which there was no historical evidence. A notable collection of eighteenth-century English and Dutch furniture has been brought together here since the 1890s. Of special interest are Chippendale-style side chairs of about 1760, an English card table, circa 1725, and a fine New England desk embellished with new carving at about the time Van Cortlandt House was first opened to the public. Atop the Dutch *kast*, or cupboard, from the Hudson River Valley, circa 1700, is a set of Delft garniture.

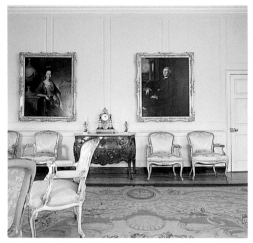

MOUNT CLARE MUSEUM HOUSE 1760

Baltimore, Maryland

Once a plantation both fertile of soil and rich in iron ore, Mount Clare's lands today are reduced to a city park in southwest Baltimore, but the green setting is still remote. The mansion was begun by Dr. Charles Carroll, who had immigrated from Ireland about 1715, and was completed in 1760 by his son Charles, known as "Barrister" Carroll. On the river facade there is a touch of Irish Georgian in the scale and restraint of the house, but the other side is wholly Maryland, with its enclosed porch room above an open porch. Wheat plantations and ironworks made the second Charles Carroll extremely wealthy, and Mount Clare, like the many other Carroll estates in Maryland, was a virtually self-sufficient paradise, with an orangery for winter fruits, orchards for summer, terraced ornamental gardens, and every diversion country life might offer. George Washington was only one of many prominent citizens who enjoyed it.

The handsomely finished interiors contain numerous Carroll furnishings, including a suite of white-painted Louis XV furniture in the drawing room. There are also Carroll portraits, the work of Charles Willson Peale, whose studies in England Carroll helped finance.

WOODVILLE, THE JOHN NEVILLE HOUSE 1789

Collier Township, Allegheny County, Pennsylvania

At the time of the American Revolution Woodville belonged to General John Neville, commander of Fort Pitt, at the head of the Ohio. He operated Woodville absentee as a farm, which he manned with slaves, and kept for himself or the overseer a house of logs. Neville actually lived not far away at his estate, Bower Hill. In 1794 whiskey rebels burned Bower Hill in an effort to ruin the unpopular Neville, who collected the loathed taxes on spirits. Neville moved to Woodville and began to expand the log house. His son Presley lived there after him, then sold the farm to his cousin Elizabeth Cowan and her husband, Christopher.

Under Elizabeth's descendants Woodville underwent some addition, but remarkably little alteration. The romantic latticed gallery was added in about 1845. Woodville developed into a house of great architectural charm, bearing the traces of time. In 1974 the heirs sold the house to the Pittsburgh History and Landmarks Foundation. Restoration to the earlier period has begun through research on paint colors that led to the brilliant green in the dining room. Original artifacts have been mixed at Woodville with distinctive regional furnishings, and archaeology is yielding information on the old garden.

DUMBARTON HOUSE 1799

Washington, D.C.

Originally named Copper Hill, then Bellevue, and since 1928 Dumbarton House, this elegant red-brick mansion was one of the galaxy of fine houses built in and around Washington when the federal government located there permanently in 1800. It is one of the few such houses that survive in the city and in 1915 was moved across the street from its original site.

Architecturally Dumbarton House is a maverick. Its rear facade recalls town houses on Boston's Beacon Hill; its tall central window is like that of its Washington contemporary, the Octagon, and those on the end facades of the White House. One is even tempted to wonder if James Hoban had a hand in the design of Dumbarton House, given its resemblances to James Monroe's Oak Hill and other work by the White House architect.

The house has had many uses since The National Society of The Colonial Dames of America acquired it in 1928 and opened its doors in the 1930s. In wartime volunteers made Red Cross bandages in its big rooms, and it has seen other community service of all kinds. As the collection of historical memorabilia kept in the house has grown, other uses have necessarily become more restricted. But Dumbarton House is not a historic house museum in the sense of being restored to represent its own history; the interiors are more generic than particular. In its rooms fine American objects of the eighteenth and nineteenth centuries are mixed in settings of a Beaux-Arts character. Since the late 1980s renovations have taken place in underground expansions that will house archives and meeting rooms, to reduce pressure on the old house.

COLONIAL DAMES
MUSEUM HOUSE 1930

New York, New York

When the architect Richard Henry Dana, Jr., completed his plan for the Colonial Dames Museum House at 215 East 71st Street, New York, in 1930, he wrote a detailed account of the historical sources for its design. His hope had been to recreate the *beau idéal* of an eighteenth-century Manhattan town house. For his facade he took that of a house, long demolished, that had stood at 34 Wall Street. Certain details came from existing places—the brick style from the Schuyler mansion at Albany; the doorway from Philipse Manor in Yonkers; the dormer windows from Stenton in Germantown, Pennsylvania; the pediment over the front door from Westover in Virginia. Inside, actual elements of old English houses, such as paneling, were incorporated in the architecture of the rooms. The result is a building of Beaux-Arts perfection that is an outstanding representation of a time when Americans were enthralled with the Anglo-Saxon past of the colonies and took great interest in British colonial architecture. Many of the houses shown in this book were restored and elaborated in the Beaux-Arts period, but the Museum House is the only example here of a house built completely new at that time.

Dana's rich and elegant interiors express not only a master's touch in the art of reusing and combining the designs of the past into harmonious architecture—for the house is magnificent to the smallest detail—but they offer a closer look even than Williamsburg at one facet of the idealization of Colonial America that came into its own in a patriotic context between World War I and the Depression.

THE OLD NORTHWEST

In the land fever that followed the American Revolution, speculators and settlers pressured the government of the Confederation for legal access to the vast domains to the northwest, which covered, it was estimated, some 250,000 square miles. Congress organized the ceded territories under a program of settlement and eventual statehood called the Northwest Ordinance, and the settlers flowed in, principally from New England and the Atlantic Seaboard. Like those who had crossed the Atlantic years before, they brought their architectural ideas with them and built several types of houses, nearly all of the simple, gabled form, but some with very handsome Federal-type detailing. With the rerouting of entry into the region over the National Road and the Erie Canal in the 1820s and 1830s, the Greek Revival made its appearance, and, as can be seen in such houses as the Clarke House in Chicago and the Lanier House in Madison, Indiana, it enjoyed a flowering in the Old Northwest in simple cottages and imposing mansions alike.

KEMPER LOG HOUSE 1804

Sharonville, Ohio

The Reverend James Kemper, a Virginian and the first Presbyterian minister ordained north of the Ohio River, built this house of squared yellow poplar logs on land he had purchased near recently settled Cincinnati. It is a substantial house, its logs joined in inverted V-notches at the corners, its front graced by a cantilevered porch, and its interior neatly chinked and smoothed. Like many log buildings, it was probably originally sheathed outside with clapboards.

Kemper's family lived for eleven years in a log blockhouse before occupying this house. General Anthony Wayne is believed to have relied on Kemper as a lookout against Indian attack, and Kemper's wife and children must have shared this responsibility, for he was often absent. He rode a three-month circuit that took him to the Northern Neck of Virginia and to Kentucky as far as the Cumberland River. He covered over two thousand miles on each trip, delivering sermons and holding services in remote places. "I missed but two appointments," he recalled of one trip. "I crossed the mountains twice, and innumerable streams, fording all of them but five. My horse came home from this joreney [sic] . . . sound and well, having carried me in this and other tours more than twenty-five thousand miles, besides doing his full share of work at home at the plough and in the carriage."

By 1912 the Kemper house was revered locally as a historic site. The Kemper family gave it up to be moved as a museum to the grounds of the Cincinnati Zoo. Forty years later it was moved to its present site in historic Sharon Woods Village. Its practical, sparsely furnished rooms bespeak the frugal character of the Kempers' pioneer life.

DAVID LENTZ HOUSE 1820

New Harmony, Indiana

This is a Harmonist house, built to specifications set by the community fathers of New Harmony. The Harmonie Society, founded earlier in the century by the Rappite sect in Württemberg, Germany, established utopian communities in Pennsylvania and this one in Indiana. The house takes its name from David Lentz, who lived here for nearly a decade as the community's only lawyer. He occupied the house with his wife, Christina, and their three sons. The house was purchased from the community in about 1840 by Thomas and Louisa Mumford, whose descendants donated the building as a museum.

As is typical of Harmonists houses, the interior spaces consist of four rooms, two up and two down, two halls, an attic, and a cellar. The outside entrance is at the side, through a garden. Houses such as this were prefabricated from lumber purchased in large quantities at low cost. Certain of the parts were cut out at a mill, numbered, and assembled on the site. The desired material was poplar because it repelled insects. Construction was post and beam, with one principal member that ran through the center of the building and supported most of the weight; the chimney, which might normally have occupied this center part, was set off center. The houses were designed for simplicity, efficiency, and permanence; but to the eye of the time, they would have appeared perhaps archaic in style.

David Lentz's house is furnished to reflect the simple tastes dictated by the Harmonists for the objects of everyday life as well as for architecture.

INDIAN AGENCY HOUSE 1832

Portage, Wisconsin

John Kinzie was appointed Indian agent at Fort Winnebago in 1829, as part of an expansion of government in this part of the Michigan territory, now Wisconsin. No resident was more hardened a pioneer than Kinzie, who had journeyed into the Northwest Territory with his parents before he was old enough to remember. He had learned Indian languages and had a strong desire to be an agent and thus champion the Indians in the encroaching migration of whites. After using temporary quarters for the agency he requested money from Congress to build a home, for he planned to marry. At last, under the patronage of Lewis Cass, $1,200 was provided. The house Kinzie built was of some stature, of milled lumber in a region of log houses.

Kinzie's wife, Juliette, was to become famous for her books about pioneer times.

In *Wau-Bun* (1856) she recalled the early 1830s, after the long Black Hawk War: "Having planted no fields during 1832...the Winnebago were in great straits for food. They crowded around the doors and windows of the new house, peering in anxiously. We were obliged to keep both doors and windows fast, to shut out the sight of misery we could not relieve." John Kinzie's pleading was finally heard by the government. "At last the boats came with the promised corn and the lawn in front of the house was a scene of wild hilarity."

Kinzie lost the struggle to protect the Winnebago lands, and Fort Winnebago was evacuated. John and Juliette moved to Chicago. Eventually the site was sold as a farm. Surrounded by the town of Portage in the twentieth century, it became a house museum.

CLARKE HOUSE MUSEUM 1836

Chicago, Illinois

One of the best examples of a Greek Revival cottage extant in the United States, the Clarke House represents a type of dwelling extremely popular in the United States from the early 1830s until the Civil War. Houses of this type were built nearly everywhere, many of them smaller, perhaps, but in general the same idea of a box structure, adorned or plain. The Clarke House, named for Henry B. Clarke, for whom it was built, is quite ornamental. It presents to the street a stagelike facade both broad and set up high, with wide front steps to the Doric portico. Houses of this kind are associated with parts of New England and with upstate New York, where so many survive. Such a relic from old Chicago is very rare.

The interior is of lofty, large rooms. A hall bisects the main floor, with rooms to the sides and a stair that rises two stories. Another stair leads up into the belvedere from which the Clarkes once surveyed the river and the thinly populated grid of early Chicago. The furnishings are not original but represent the period 1840 to about 1865 in a variety of mahogany modes called "Grecian" then, "Empire" today, as well as cottage pieces such as spool tables and rocking chairs.

Within the past two decades the house was threatened with demolition. Its rescue included a move, and the move's path was obstructed by a freeway bridge. Undaunted, the restorers jacked the house up the height of the bridge, rolled it across, and lowered it to grade again to complete its trip to an architectural park.

KILBOURNTOWN HOUSE 1844

Milwaukee, Wisconsin

The temple-style house of Benjamin Church, master builder, is a direct import from central New York, Church's home. The Doric portico, with its fluted columns, gives importance and Grecian style to an otherwise simple cottage, decorated within at the cornices, windows, and doors. (Church brought the millwork, which was made in Buffalo, with him to Wisconsin.) Like the exterior, the plan is typical of Greek Revival houses of the time in New York state, featuring a side-wing kitchen and dining room with porches. The rooms are small-scale, but the ceilings are high.

Benjamin Church migrated to Wisconsin in the 1840s. His fortunes improved in Milwaukee, and in the census of 1860 he listed himself as a gentleman. Kilbourntown's furnishings, which include many pieces of Wisconsin provenance, harmonize with the Greek Revival architecture. Among them is a table by Ernst Hagen, the Milwaukee work of a New York cabinetmaker who, like Church himself, set up shop in Wisconsin. The table was made about 1857, during the brief period of Hagen's residence outside New York.

In 1939 the house was moved from its original location to Estabrook Park in Milwaukee. It was restored after long years of virtual abandon. It was seriously damaged by fire in 1970 and once again restored on the basis of detailed research. As the home of a master builder, Kilbourntown is of special interest as a house museum.

J. F. D. LANIER
STATE HISTORIC SITE 1844

Madison, Indiana

The architect of the Lanier mansion was Francis Costigan, who came from a Baltimore intoxicated with the Greek Revival to build this house on the Ohio River. In ornamentation and dramatic effects the Lanier House is very grand. Much of the detailing can be found illustrated in Minard Lafever's *Beauties of Modern Architecture*, the most fashionable manual on Greek Revival architecture in print at the time. The client, the wealthy lawyer and banker James Franklin Doughty Lanier, was willing to lavish money on the house, and Costigan designed it with flair.

The Lanier House rises three stories over a basement. The plan is a hybrid. It is like the usual center-hall Greek Revival in the placement of its main rooms, yet the circular staircase is introduced into the hall halfway down, breaking up the usual sweep. A side service wing makes the plan similar to those of Greek Revival cottages in central and upstate New York.

The family retained its wealth, so the house was improved in the generations that followed the builder. Alexander Lanier, in the second generation, added stylish Néo-Grec wall decorations to parts of the house and a mansard roof to the side service wing. The elder Lanier had brought many comforts to his house, including central heating and gaslight; the lantern on the roof was in fact part of a ventilating system for summer.

The house passed from the family into state hands in 1925, when it was still at a relatively young age. Many of its original furnishings remain in the rooms, and others of the years 1844 to about 1880 have been added to replace those the family took with them.

COMMANDER'S RESIDENCE, HISTORIC FORT WAYNE 1880

Detroit, Michigan

The federal government established Fort Wayne in 1842 and held it until 1971, when it was converted into the Historic Fort Wayne Museum Complex. Among the buildings that served Fort Wayne for a third of its nearly 130 years was the Commander's Residence, designed and built in 1880 by Lieutenant Alexander Perry of the Army Quartermaster Corps. The first occupants of the house were Colonel Henry Boynton Clitz and his family, and the restoration, completed in 1985, reflects his tenure of several years.

Research in photographic archives of the army proved definitive in the re-creation of the Victorian rooms, with their Aesthetic affectations. Special attention was paid to the transient nature of life in these military houses. Documentary photographs of interiors typically show numbers of small objects—curiosities, memorabilia, home art, and fancy things. Some of the objects that decorate the Commander's Residence are authentic, and others are copies of known originals, but the desired effect of clutter is achieved admirably. Sets or partial sets of fashionable mass-produced walnut furniture find places in the rooms beside odd tables and chairs. The fresh, bright wallpapers are the sort that each successive family might have added, ordering this product through the mail from catalogs. Fancy wall-to-wall carpeting, similarly available, might also have come from the extensive markets of Detroit mercantile houses in the 1880s. In the kitchen the cast-iron Detroit Jewel range is a plausible substitute for the original.

THE OLD SOUTHWEST

The country of Daniel Boone and Andrew Jackson was settled just after the Revolution, at a time when Indian opposition to white intrusion was frequent and fierce. Kentucky was claimed by Virginia and Tennessee by North Carolina, both claims overturned in the 1790s when the regions became territories, then states. Louisiana entered the Union as a territory in 1802 with Jefferson's land purchase from Napoleon. The area called the Florida Parishes—extending from Pensacola on the Gulf to Saint Francisville on the Mississippi—was not part of the purchase and came under the American flag only in 1819. From the early French towns on the Mississippi River in Missouri south to New Orleans, the region was linked by inland areas dependent on the access the Great River gave to the sea. At the time of the Anglo-American immigration, Louisiana and, to a lesser extent, Missouri, already had established populations of Europeans, some Creoles and some transplanted French Canadians. The early architecture of the Old Southwest was among the most varied anywhere on the continent, a mixture of French and Spanish in Louisiana and Missouri and Anglo-American in Kentucky and Tennessee. Eventually the latter dominated, but the regional flavoring remained to give a unique character to the nineteenth century's succession of styles.

LOUIS BOLDUC HOUSE 1775

Ste. Genevieve, Missouri

Louis Bolduc was a French Canadian who migrated to the Illinois country, settling here at Ste. Genevieve on the Mississippi River and enjoying a long life as a prosperous planter, lead miner, and owner of a store, which was also a sort of trading post. His French-speaking household was numerous in family, Indian servants, and black slaves.

The Louis Bolduc House is of premier interest architecturally among all the existing French colonial buildings in the United States today. In form it has much in common with Louisiana's Kent Plantation House (see pp. 162–165), but it is set much lower to the ground. It is also very similar to the Louisiana house in construction: the oak frame is in-filled with plaster, or *bousillage*, made of mud, Spanish moss, and animal hair. One can but marvel at the majestic timber frame, the heavy oak trusses held together by mortises and tenons. The steep roof is shingled, where in colder climates it might have been thatched. Archaeology has shown that the surrounding lot was palisaded, with fenced areas within for animals and gardens. Bolduc's granddaughter Agathe, married to René Le Meilleur, later built a house on the property, beside the early house, and this too is preserved.

The interior was originally two large rooms, each some thirty feet square with large fireplaces. In later times one of these was subdivided into a hallway and a smaller room. A stone kitchen was partitioned off the surrounding gallery. Today the furniture consists of Canadian and French pieces of the period of the house and objects that actually belonged to the family, which lived here until the 1940s.

LIBERTY HALL 1796

Frankfort, Kentucky

One of many architectural jewels in Kentucky's capital is Liberty Hall, the home of Kentucky's first United States senator. It is perhaps the classic expression of the "Kentucky Federal" style, that often whimsical variation on the red-brick Georgian vernacular of Virginia and New England that is in fact the antithesis of the thin-skinned Federal mode. There is a certain innocence in the spare wooden elements and Georgian solidity of this house.

Senator John Brown, the leading figure in Kentucky politics before the rise of Henry Clay, built this house overlooking the Kentucky River soon after Frankfort became the state capital. To the barny interior John and Margaretta Brown brought the best of everything in furnishings, china, and glassware. Among the callers at Liberty Hall was General Lafayette, who was on his American tour in 1825. By this time the Browns had withdrawn from an active social life, in keeping with their religious professions of recent date. Margaretta, eager to see the Hero of Two Worlds, hesitated when weaker souls urged her to break her pledge to avoid any "place of public amusement." But she stayed behind when her friends left for the ball where the general was to appear. No sooner had they gone, she wrote, "when who should arrive here but Gen'l Lafayette, his son and suite. The General spent an hour with us in the most delightful conversation, while those who went to the ball did not exchange a syllable with him. Had I not a triumph?"

KENT PLANTATION HOUSE 1796

Alexandria, Louisiana

Probably the last surviving example of Creole-style architecture in central Louisiana, Kent Plantation House was built at the close of the eighteenth century by a Creole, Pierre Baillio II, and expanded a half-century later by a subsequent Anglo-American owner, Robert Cruikshank Hynson. The architectural vernacular is that of the tropics, with a row of breezy rooms raised up on piers high above the ground; in such houses the upper floor is of wood or mud "cats" on lath that dry easily, while the supporting structure is brick. Kent Plantation House gleams white, paint today, perhaps whitewash long ago, and surveys the roses and sunflowers of the yard.

The house was moved a short distance from its original site in 1964 and restored as a plantation museum. The interiors boast a fine collection of locally made furnishings and pieces of the sort that might have been brought in from New Orleans and in some cases even New York. Kent Plantation was located some ninety miles from the Mississippi River, to which it had access over the nearby Red River. Its crops moved by raft, flatboat, keelboat, and later by steamboat, and in the same way city goods were returned to this remote place. In restoration an effort has been made to show what might have been typical, rather than attempting a recreation of the houses of Baillio or Hynson. In the dining room the punkah, or fly fan, hangs over a mahogany table. Books with handsome leather bindings fill a cypress bookcase. The comfortable galleries might, but for the invention of air conditioning, still be part of Louisiana life.

OAKLEY PLANTATION HOUSE 1799

St. Francisville, Louisiana

Oakley plantation was established on 700 arpents of land in Spanish West Florida in 1799. Its owner, Ruffin Gray, died within a few years, leaving his interests to his widow, Lucretia Alston Gray, who increased Oakley by 1,000 acres and made its rich, rolling plantation one of the best in the Felicianas, as the hilly region of West Florida was called. In 1803 she married James Pierre, an official of the Spanish government. In 1821, when their daughter Eliza was in her teens and West Florida had been American for three years, they engaged John James Audubon as tutor at Oakley, under a contract specifying that he would have time to wander the woods in search of bird subjects to paint. Here, where he lived for four months, the naturalist painted thirty-two of the birds in his *Birds of America*.

Oakley remained in the family until 1947. It is one of the most hauntingly beautiful of Louisiana houses, three full stories, with triple galleries; inside it is two rooms across, with three rooms behind those. The house is of frame in its upper two stories. As is typical of Louisiana houses, the walls and floors of the ground floor are brick. Life at Oakley centered during most of the year in the galleries. In hot months beds could be drawn out on the top gallery, where louvers gave privacy and protection from frequent rains. The rooms are furnished with objects stylish at the time Audubon was there. Lamps, candle holders, and other household objects are found in the outdoor kitchen house, with its unglazed windows. The walnut punkah over the dining room table is original to the house and perhaps to the time of Audubon's visit.

TRAVELLERS REST HISTORIC HOUSE MUSEUM 1799, 1828

Nashville, Tennessee

The rambling house of Judge John Overton captures the spirit of early settlement in the late eighteenth- and early nineteenth-century Cumberland River region of Tennessee. Built in parts over thirty years, the house reflects Overton's life from his pioneer days as a young lawyer to his eventual rise to political power-broker status in Jacksonian America. In his youth Overton left Virginia for Kentucky and then moved to Tennessee, where he met Andrew Jackson and Rachel Donelson Robards, who was to be Jackson's wife. While Jackson rose in politics, Overton became a rich man through his interests in land and banking. He was an ardent promoter of his friend and the person closest to the truth about Jackson's shadowed marriage, which became a major campaign issue.

Overton built his plantation house on this plantation in 1799, atop an Indian burial mound he called Golgotha, for all the skulls unearthed when he dug his cellar. Hard years on the road as a circuit judge caused him to change the name to Travellers Rest. By 1808 he was able to enlarge the house, adding several rooms to the left side. In 1828, married to the amiable widow Mary White May Overton, he built a large brick ell to the wooden house, making the side into a new front with a deep porch. The interior was decorated in 1829, including wallpaper of bright yellow—the same color President Jackson used in the East Room in the same year—and two pier tables Overton purchased in Philadelphia. Overton died at Travellers Rest in 1833, and his descendants occupied the farm for a century. It became a museum in the 1950s.

HERMANN-GRIMA
HISTORIC HOUSE 1831

New Orleans, Louisiana

This handsome city house was built for Samuel and Marie Amaranth Hermann during an opulent era in New Orleans history, a period that helped define architecturally the city we know today. Samuel Hermann contracted with a builder named William Brand to erect the house. The result was a large and handsome brick house which in plan a proper New Orleanian would have called *américaine;* its long central hall, flanked by rooms, was not in the Creole tradition, which forsook halls in favor of rooms that opened one into another. Otherwise the house is not exceptional in its environs, the new influence of the Greek Revival very evident in its interior columns, trim, and other details. The rear loggia and its flanking *cabinets* are all typical of New Orleans.

A restoration in the 1970s drew on rich documentation that provided details of the elegant house occupied by the Hermanns. Greek Revival period furniture, some original to the Hermanns, is used in all the rooms. Other pieces, fewer in number, such as the grand *lit de parade* with its draped half-tester, reflect the Rococo Revival of the 1840s and 1850s. Gaslight is mixed with candles and lamplight, though gas was the predominant lighting of the era. Wall-to-wall carpeting covers most of the pine flooring. In the kitchen is a brick *potager*, a kind of range that would have been familiar to Spanish and French residents and less so to Anglos. Fueled by wood fires from below, such ranges were equipped with grills to cook on and "stue holes" in which deep pots were set to heat water. Such devices were replaced by the iron range about the time this house was built.

ORLANDO BROWN HOUSE 1835

Frankfort, Kentucky

The architect of the Orlando Brown House, Gideon Shyrock, had designed the Kentucky statehouse only a few years before, and in so doing created one of the major monuments to the Greek Revival in the United States. The mansion he designed for the lawyer and editor Orlando Brown, however, reaches back into a red-brick and wood-trim Federal mode that was popular in various forms in Kentucky from the late 1790s until the Civil War, and is seen in Brown's father's house, Liberty Hall (see pp. 158–161), which is next door. The version used in Orlando Brown's house is more ornamental than usual, with Grecian embellishments.

Orlando Brown's life was often restless. The death of his young wife in 1841 left him devastated, with children to rear. At times he tried living in places other than Frankfort, but he always returned. His friend Washington Irving hoped that he would settle down at home and write of old Kentucky as Irving had written of old New York. But fiction did not interest Brown as much as journalism, and his newspaper, *The Frankfort Commonwealth*, was widely read beyond Kentucky for the excellence of his writing.

After his death, just after the Civil War, his heirs remained in the house for two more generations before bequeathing it for use as a historic house museum. Except for some Colonial Revival alterations made by the family, the house has changed little and retains a rich collection of family memorabilia.

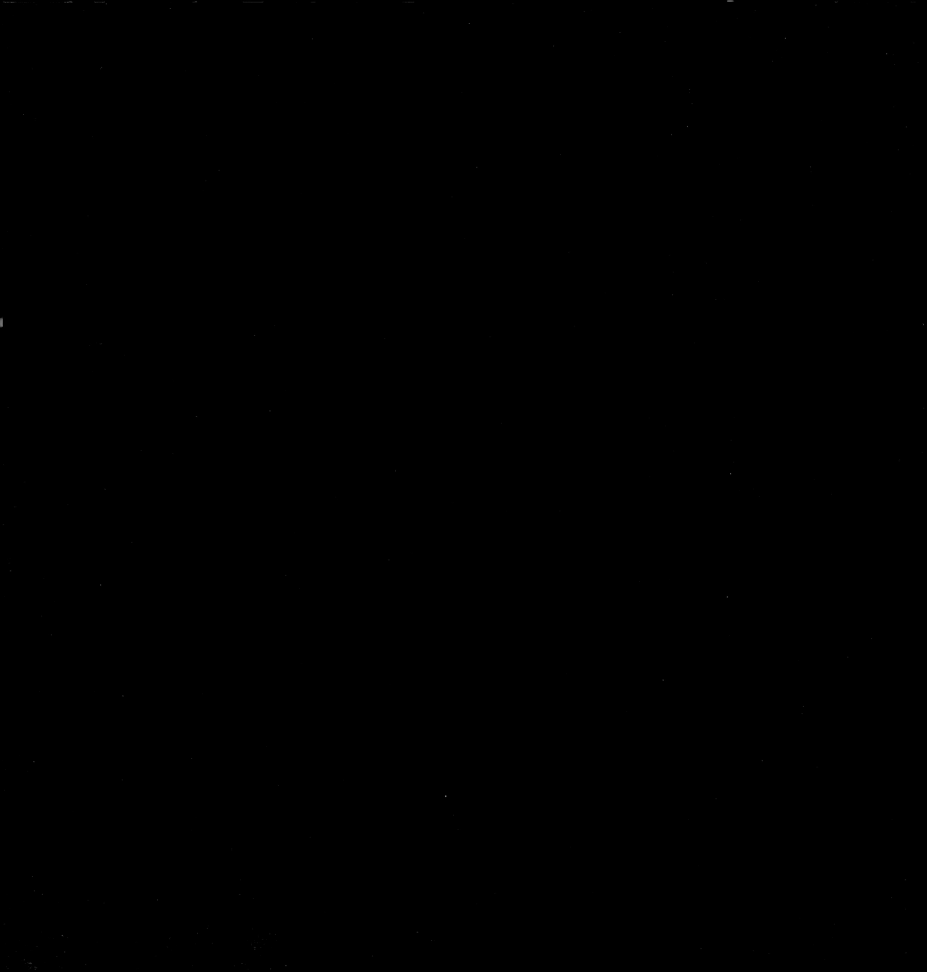

THE SOUTH

The South defined here is not the Confederate South, but the coastal, or "lower," South: Georgia, Florida, Alabama, Mississippi, and on west to central Texas. (Louisiana, because of its earlier history, is considered part of the Old Southwest.) Georgia, Florida, and Mississippi have earlier dates of settlement than the rest. The Ximenez-Fatio House in Saint Augustine recalls the later Spanish period, and Evansview-Bontura House in Natchez is believed to have been built in 1790 when Natchez was in British hands. Inland along the rivers the Spanish, French, and British built farmhouses, forts, and outposts with stores, and their architectural characteristics exercised some local authority in the later Anglo-American domination. Most of the houses shown here give less the general picture than a particular classical image of the prosperous antebellum years.

EVANSVIEW-BONTURA HOUSE 1790

Natchez, Mississippi

Robert D. Smith, a successful free black businessman, built this house in stages between 1851 and 1858 as a combination residence and work place. The simple Greek Revival town house form was altered by subsequent owners, who, in the 1890s, replaced the one-story wooden porch with a two-story porch with frothy Ohio-made ironwork. Smith, who had moved to Natchez from Maryland, purchased the land in 1851 for $500, and after he had, according to the laws of Mississippi, proved to the state authorities that he was of good character, was granted a license as a "free man of color" to satisfy the law and to protect himself and his family from kidnapping and sale into slavery.

Smith prospered in a culture which, on the law books, at least, seemed hostile to free blacks. He was a hackman—a hauler and "taxi" driver—when he arrived in 1843, and in 1849 he opened a livery stable, which he moved to this riverfront site high on the bluffs three years later. Business was good in this location near the Mississippi River docks. He added to his new house in 1854 and died here in 1858, leaving his widow, Ann, a woman of means. She remained until the eve of the Civil War, when, foreseeing danger in her situation as a free black woman, she took her children to Chile, to join an elder son, who had opened a foundry in Valparaiso. In the 1940s the house was restored by Mr. and Mrs. Hugh Hinton Evans and given 1840s and 1850s furnishings typical of antebellum Natchez.

XIMENEZ-FATIO HOUSE 1798

Saint Augustine, Florida

The Spanish settlement of Saint Augustine was more than two centuries old when this house was built by Andres Ximenez, a merchant and native of Granada in Spain. The original building consisted of the large front part, which Ximenez operated downstairs as a tavern, with living space above and a long rear wing of warehouses for his stores. Probably late in the 1820s, when Florida had become a state, it was converted to a hotel or boardinghouse, and probably in the 1830s its warehouses were made two-story and rebuilt inside as hotel rooms; outside, enclosed wooden galleries on the patio served as corridors.

In the 1930s the house began life as a museum house featuring its Spanish past, but in the 1970s its focus was changed to tell a later story of a succession of women, notably Louisa Fatio, who operated it as a winter hotel. Guests—nearly always deathly ill—sailed here from the cold climates to enjoy the warm air and citrus fruits, the charming foreignness of Saint Augustine, and not least the famous dining rooms such as that of Louisa Fatio. The hotel slept about twenty. Some brought their coffins along, the lucky ones, health restored, to sell them jubilantly at the end of the season.

Within the thick coquina stone walls of the house the original Spanish style yielded early on to Greek Revival wood trim, fireplaces, carved mahogany furniture, Brussels carpeting, and other expressions of Anglo-American taste. Still, the old flavor survives in the shady porches, the rose-washed plaster walls, and the tangled garden of palms, fruit trees, shrubbery, and vines, which is fragrant and green all winter.

CONDÉ-CHARLOTTE MUSEUM HOUSE 1822

Mobile, Alabama

Part of the thick foundation of this house was built for an earlier house in 1711, taking it back to the time when the Mobile area was under French rule. The present house was built in the 1820s and given its two-story porch just before 1850. Parts of the French Fort Condé still stood on the site in the 1840s, and a Vermont builder named Peter Hobart erected this building after it was destroyed, using part of the old powder magazine. A subsequent owner, Jonathan Kirkbride, remodeled the house into a modern residence, and it stayed in his family until 1926. In 1957 it became a house museum. The rooms represent the various historical periods of government in Mobile—French, English, early American, and Confederate. The double parlor, with its Rococo Revival furniture and gilded gas chandeliers, represents the Civil War era. Garden and galleries are furnished with plants representing the Spanish period.

ANDREW LOW HOUSE 1848

Savannah, Georgia

This Tuscan villa of 1848 was built by a transplanted Scotsman, Andrew Low, who was drawn to Savannah by the flourishing antebellum cotton business. His rise to wealth through inheritance from a rich uncle was relatively quick, and the mansion in which he established himself on Lafayette Square reflected his prosperity. The architect, John Norris of New York, gave Low a stylish, modern house, of stucco on brick. The interior is Greek Revival in its architectural details, with richly decorated doorways and large expanses of plaster which Low undoubtedly had papered. Norris adjusted the design to the hot climate with long windows and french doors and a long ironwork tribunal along the street that gave shade to the parlors and made it possible to leave windows open in the rain. All the windows had louvered blinds, and the two-story rear galleries were completely enclosed with them.

Low and his wife, Sarah, went to England to buy furniture, and on their return she died. Not until his remarriage to Elizabeth Stiles in 1854 did the house come into its own as a social center. William Thackeray visited twice, admiring the "pretty wife" and noting that life was "a feast every day." By the close of the Civil War Low was a widower again, with a house that no longer interested him. Robert E. Lee visited in 1870 and found the house "partially dismantled." When Low died the house and a fortune of three millions passed to his only son, William Mackay Low, whose wife, Julia Magill Gordon, founded the Girl Scouts of America there in 1912.

THE OAKS 1853

Jackson, Mississippi

This small vernacular cottage, with its sparse Greek Revival detailing, is probably as generically American as any house in this book. It was the home of James H. Boyd, a druggist, real estate investor, and eventually owner of steamboats on the Pearl River. He served in public offices, and he and his wife, Eliza Ellis Boyd, reared six children in this house, which was probably not unlike many other houses along the streets of Mississippi's capital.

The cottage measures forty-seven by thirty-four feet and has four rooms separated by a central hallway ten feet wide. Originally the domestic services were contained in outbuildings, including a kitchen, stable, workrooms, and a privy.

Only the dairy survives, with its brick-lined pool in the center of the floor. In the twentieth century a rear wing, which remains, was built to serve the domestic functions that remained on the site.

The Oaks remained in the original family until 1960, when it became a house museum, so it was possible to locate and return some furnishings to the house. These have been mixed with objects typical of such houses in the 1850s. The heavy, architectural furniture seems to suit the tall rooms perfectly. Most of it is "Grecian," such as the great bed of about 1850 and the dining room's original sideboard. In the yard, surrounded by a picket fence, old oaks and magnolias shade typical southern plantings of cape jasmine, crêpe myrtle, azalea, camellia, and quince.

NEILL-COCHRAN MUSEUM HOUSE 1855

Austin, Texas

The Neill-Cochran House was built for Washington L. Hill but carries the names of later owners, Colonel Andrew Neill and Judge T. B. Cochran. It is one in a series of Greek Revival houses of about the same date in the Texas capital, a phenomenon the restoration architect Ernest A. Connally called "architecture at the end of the South," referring to the surprising appearance of deep-South characteristics just where the geographical South dramatically ends and the Great Plains begin. All the buildings in the group are attributed to Abner Cook, a builder who had lived for a while in Alabama and eventually settled in Austin. A Richard Payne served Cook on occasion as designer, relying, as late as the 1850s, on the pattern books of Asher Benjamin. His hand in the Neill-Cochran House is a possibility.

The house is built of native limestone, not cut in ashlar blocks, as it often was, but in odd quarry sizes, more like rock. The effect is a rough finish typical of the area. What makes the house exceptional is the file of twenty-six foot columns in wood that crosses its entire front. They were made of pine brought from the nearest forests, those of Bastrop, fifty miles east. Pine woodwork and staircase complete the plaster-walled interior.

The house was used for many purposes in its early days, notably, from 1857, as an asylum for the blind. Under the Cochran tenure many modernizations were made, including a new front door and surround, hardwood floors, and a rear wing. As a museum house since 1958, the Neill-Cochran House has been furnished with objects dating generally from the 1850s to the 1920s.

RANKIN HOUSE 1850-1870

Columbus, Georgia

The James Rankin House, begun before the Civil War, was the finest house in Columbus, Georgia, for at least a half-century. It was the home of a Scot, a cotton planter, who did not complete its construction until 1865, and its furnishing and finishing probably not until about 1870. The Italianate house, fronted by an elegant ironwork piazza, presents a grand appearance to the street, but its interior is even more imposing, with fine, large rooms, niches for statuary, marble mantelpieces, and a splendid divided staircase.

Columbus was a wealthy town in the nineteenth century, as today, with a mix of agrarian and manufacturing interests to keep the economy diversified. The poverty that followed the Civil War in many areas of the South was not as evident here. The Rankin house has been restored to reflect the life of a wealthy citizen of Columbus from the 1850s to the 1870s. Some original Rankin furnishings have been brought back, and the setting has been enhanced with reproduction carpeting, window hangings, and a wide variety of types of lighting fixtures. The house is a museum house, but it is also used for community events such as meetings, receptions, and weddings.

CLARA BARKLEY DORR HOUSE 1871

Pensacola, Florida

A Gulf Coast house type had been long established in such houses as Mobile's Fort Condé-Charlotte House when the widow Clara Barkley Dorr built this wooden house in 1871. With its classic side-hall plan, double parlors, and long windows it could as easily have been built in the 1820s as the 1870s. The interiors are not restored but recreated in a generic sense to represent the region in the post–Civil War years. Original side chairs in the parlor join a large supporting cast of Victorian antiques, with copies of historical wallpapers, using borders typical of the period. Kerosene chandeliers authentic to the period are designed to resemble gas chandeliers, an artifice common at the time. The pine floors are polished, as became a custom when wall-to-wall carpeting went out of style in the 1870s and 1880s.

THE MIDWEST

What we call the Midwest today is made up in part from the Northwest Territory east of the Mississippi River and in part of lands from the Louisiana Purchase, including the states immediately west of the Mississippi: Iowa, Minnesota, and Missouri. (Missouri's venerable French town of Ste. Genevieve is extracted and included as part of the Old Southwest, where it belongs historically.) The architecture of the Midwest did not come into its real flowering until the late nineteenth century with Chicago's sky-scrapers and the emergence of the Prairie Style. In the years of settlement and the first half-century of statehood, midwestern architecture tended to be imitative of that in other areas, and its character was often shaped by a certain solidity and austerity, as in Plum Grove in Iowa City and the John Wornall House in Kansas City. Change began to come immediately after the Civil War with the dramatic rise in building monumental public structures—notably new state capitols and county courthouses—and their influence on houses such as the Alexander Ramsey House in Saint Paul.

PLUM GROVE 1845

Iowa City, Iowa

Plum Grove, a Greek Revival house which nevertheless seems Federal in its proportions and restraint, was built by Robert Lucas, first territorial governor of Iowa. Born in what is now West Virginia at Shepherdstown, he moved as a young man to Ohio, where he enjoyed a distinguished political career, ultimately serving as governor. He was appointed territorial governor of Iowa by President Martin Van Buren in 1838, but when he left, his wife, Friendly Sumner Lucas, refused to accompany him, preferring to remain at their Ohio farm, which she called Friendly Grove. Six years passed, and Lucas's success in Iowa, together with the realization that he had no political prospects in Ohio or in Washington, convinced him that he must remain. He finally was able to coax Friendly to see Iowa and she liked it. The result was Plum Grove, completed in 1844. Built of red Iowa City brick, it consists of a two-story house and a kitchen house.

The tall governor and the five-foot, two-hundred-pound Friendly settled into their house with what appears to have been a mixture of types of furnishings bought new and brought from Ohio. Still in the house today are an Empire-type sofa, a desk, and a straight side chair that belonged to them. The house has been kept simple, as it was, with floors largely bare and a farmhouse character to the sparsely furnished rooms. Here the governor lived for only nine years; his wife survived him by nearly twenty.

CODY-McCAUSLAND HOUSE 1847, 1870

Davenport, Iowa

The boyhood home of Colonel William F. Cody, known as Buffalo Bill, was built by his father in 1847 on 7,000 acres of virgin land. It is a two-story house, a classic example of the "I house" form—one room deep, three rooms wide, and associated with Midwestern states whose names begin with the letter I—in this case built of fieldstone. The woodwork inside, including the floors, is entirely of walnut, cut from large trees on the land and milled nearby. It was the Codys' home for only three years, before the father, Isaac, packed them all up and headed by wagon train to Kansas. The house was purchased by members of the McCausland family, and in 1870 they added a frame section that almost doubled its size.

In 1967 it was decided to make the house a museum. By that time William Cody, as Buffalo Bill, had long been a figure in American legend. He had grown up to be a famous frontier scout, and then, at the World's Columbian Exposition in Chicago in 1893, he introduced his Wild West Show, which traveled the world. As its star, Buffalo Bill thrilled a generation of Americans by bringing his audiences death-defying acts, super skills, and Great Plains spectacles beneath the circus tent.

The Cody-McCausland House is restored to represent the days when it was young. Cottage furniture, some of it painted, finds a familiar setting in the big, square rooms, along with lace curtains, painted shades, and fancy Victorian wallpapers. Most of the furniture was used locally, although none of it belonged to Buffalo Bill.

CAMPBELL HOUSE 1851

St. Louis, Missouri

One of America's most famous town houses, the mid-nineteenth-century mansion of Robert and Virginia Campbell is representative of the dwellings of wealthy residents of St. Louis before the Civil War. It was a flush time, when St. Louis was the sister city to New Orleans on a Mississippi River busy with steamboat traffic. Campbell, a native of Ireland, came to America at the age of 18 and began clerking in various mercantile houses. Opportunity attracted him to St. Louis, gateway to the West, where he entered the business of selling supplies to immigrant parties heading to unsettled country. He eventually made his fortune and married. He and Virginia Campbell had several St. Louis houses before building this one.

The house is a side-hall detached row house of great size. The parlor that runs along the left of the hall was furnished in richly carved "French antique" suites in dark mahogany covered with silk, all imitating the Louis XV style. Elaborate gilt bronze chandeliers burned gas, and the light fell on white marble mantelpieces, lace curtains, and luxuriously colored Brussels carpeting.

The family quarters upstairs boasted a bathroom, as well as finely appointed bedrooms, featuring carved beds, bureaux, and tall wardrobes. Over nearly a century the Campbell heirs occupied the house, until early in World War II, when it became a museum. One of the earliest Victorian house museums in the country, the Campbell House is a special treasure because of its almost entirely original furnishings and accessories.

JOHN WORNALL HOUSE 1858

Kansas City, Missouri

The John Wornall House originally stood on a plantation, but now it is in a city neighborhood, with only its yard to hint of its rural origins. An austere, late Greek Revival house fronted by tall box columns, or piers, it has the usual plan of center hall and flanking rooms. The builder, John Wornall, journeyed to Kansas as a boy with his parents and in 1843 settled on the 500 acres on which the house was to be built. On this farm his parents raised cattle, sheep, and grain crops. They did a thriving trade with settlers and wagon trains headed west on the Santa Fe Trail. In 1849, when his mother died and his father returned to Kentucky, John Wornall assumed title to the farm. After his second marriage, Wornall decided to build a fine house.

The best standards of the time would have judged the house plain, but it was pretentious for its location. The design probably came from pattern books of the day. Wornall furnished it well, with such conveniences as oil lamps and modern heating stoves. During the Civil War the Wornall house was occupied by soldiers of both armies. Mrs. Wornall later recalled cooking in the rear-wing kitchen for Union and Confederate soldiers before the Battle of Westport in October 1864. When the house was restored in 1964 by the Jackson County Historical Society, it was decided to keep it as much as possible as the Wornalls had had it, but to also make it a mirror of life in the Civil War period in the area around Kansas City. The result is a fine collection of regional furniture—much of it made elsewhere but used here—and memorabilia of the Wornall family.

FLYNN MANSION 1870

Des Moines, Iowa

Martin Flynn, born in Ireland, came to America and made money clearing rights-of-way for railroad companies. In 1867, while yet only twenty-six, he purchased 600 acres of farmland outside Des Moines and three years later began construction of a large, round-arched Italianate house of brick. He called it and the farm Walnut Hill, but his wife Ellen quickly nicknamed the house "The Brick." It had large, airy rooms and halls, with walnut trim and tall windows. Flynn purchased his furniture on the popular market of the time, acquiring marble-topped tables and bedroom and dining room sets. The farm prospered as a cattle ranch, although Martin Flynn's principal income came from other sources. His personal interest lay in the raising and sale of shorthorn cattle, and annual cattle sales at the farm drew people from many states. Flynn died in 1906, and the farm left his family in 1915.

In 1970, its land intact, the Flynn farm and its ramshackle mansion became a living history farm, and the land and outbuildings as well as the house itself were restored. The rooms evoke the era of the Flynns in the nineteenth century; comfortable Victorian furnishings are seen in a context of wallpapers, carpeting, and other decorations appropriate to the time. Some Flynn family furnishings have been returned to the house, as well as objects from other old Iowa houses.

ALEXANDER RAMSEY HOUSE 1872

St. Paul, Minnesota

Begun in the late 1860s, the house of Alexander Ramsey was completed in 1872 and served his family for ninety-two years, at last being bequeathed to the Minnesota Historical Society intact by his granddaughters in 1964. When the Ramsey House, filled with original family possessions, entered the museum world in the 1960s it had a profound effect nationally on interest in Victorian houses and customs and helped establish the Midwest as a major source of artifacts and resource for study in the field of late nineteenth-century decorative arts.

Ramsey was territorial governor of Minnesota in 1849 and stayed on after statehood to become a leader in business in the growing St. Paul community. Monroe Sheire of St. Paul was his architect, and Ramsey chose the popular Americanization of the French Second Empire for the style; it was to be a formal house, but a family house as well. The plan followed the traditional arrangement of center hall with parlor to one side and library and a smaller parlor on the other. Service rooms and dining room were in a rear wing. The house is of native limestone, cut in small blocks, and most of the trim is pine. Within, the woodwork is grained with paint to resemble a variety of woods: oak, maple, butternut. The large parlor is not unlike that in the Campbell House in St. Louis, with its two marble mantelpieces and the deep bay in between for plants. Anna Ramsey selected most of the furniture in the year the house was completed, and the original furniture and carpeting are still there, with wallpaper reproduced from existing fragments.

THE WEST

This is the West of romance, from the years of the Santa Fe Trail to the era of Billy the Kid. After a long and complex history under Spain, then Mexico, Anglo-American settlement accelerated after the Mexican War, spurred on by gold and silver strikes that supplied clients for the Hotel de Paris in Georgetown, Colorado, and by the cattle business, as well as by the discovery in the twentieth century of seemingly bottomless pools of oil. Notable here are several adobe structures, each of a different sort, from the very earliest, the seventeenth-century Spanish Palace of the Governors at Santa Fe, to the Victorian John C. Frémont House in Tucson. Brick or frame houses made their appearance after the opening up of the West by the railroad, on which building supplies and population rolled to lands once barely accessible. With the train cars came ideas and tastes current in the Midwest and, perhaps to a lesser extent, on the east coast. The houses here show a progression in the architecture of the West to the beginning of the twentieth century, a movement from the pioneer vernacular of the Mandel Post Office to styles, like that of the great brick Overholser Mansion, that could be called national.

PALACE OF THE GOVERNORS 1610

Santa Fe, New Mexico

A list of the ten most historic buildings in the United States would have to include the Palace of the Governors on the plaza at Santa Fe. The long, low, rambling adobe structure symbolized and housed Spanish administrative authority for more than 200 years and still recalls vividly the days of Spanish and Mexican rule on the frontier of New Spain.

Archaeology has shown that the palace began relatively small and grew more or less room by room into a public building of large size, its rooms opening inside onto a large central patio that gave space to wagons, animals, household services, gardening, and a variety of other tenants and functions. The rooms are lofty, with wooden ceilings atop which about a foot of dirt formed the original roof. A mud plaster or cotton cloth was often used to keep the dirt from sifting down. Ox blood was poured on the packed floors to keep the dust in place. The walls were washed in various colors, together with whitewash.

In its Spanish and Mexican days the rooms were sparse, with simple wooden furniture; the officials who lived there probably brought with them great wooden chests filled with textiles, brass, silver, porcelain, and accoutrements for worship. General Lew Wallace, who wrote *Ben-Hur* in the palace while he was territorial governor in the 1870s, remembered a house that felt ancient, with ceilings as soot-layered "as those of Cedric the Saxon." Today the palace is carefully maintained and the subject of ongoing research. It houses restored rooms as well as a collection of artifacts from the Spanish colonial period contributed by The National Society of The Colonial Dames of America in New Mexico.

JOHN C. FRÉMONT HOUSE MUSEUM circa 1860

Tucson, Arizona

When President Rutherford B. Hayes appointed John C. Frémont governor of the Arizona territory in 1878, he was giving Arizona as its chief official the West's most legendary living hero. Frémont, "the pathfinder," had been in the forefront of expansion during the 1840s, and later, as a celebrity, ran for president. By 1878 the fortune he had made in California gold was lost, and Frémont was in financial difficulties. He moved to Tucson with his wife, Jessie Benton Frémont, and their daughter, Elizabeth. They occupied this house for three years while Frémont served as governor.

It is a house of adobe, thick-walled, with *vigas*, or exposed joists of pine, supporting a *savinas* ceiling, which is made variously of saguaro cactus, ocotillo bushes, or carrizo reeds that keep the deep dirt layer of roofing from sifting down into the living area. The everyday living room is a central hall with doors at each end; it opens at the rear onto a walled patio shaded by an ancient fig tree, grown to enormous size. Small windows and tall doorways send shafts of light into the dark, thick-walled rooms, which Jessie Frémont papered in artistic Victorian patterns and decorated with Indian pots. In the dining room Frémont's sword hangs below an engraving of him made long before he lived here, at the sunset of his career as the man who was always on the spot in the opening of the West.

FORT LOWELL MUSEUM 1873, 1963

Tucson, Arizona

The commanding officer's quarters at Fort Lowell were reconstructed in 1963 following federal records of the original, built in 1873. Fort Lowell was established elsewhere in the region of Tucson as Camp Lowell and, having been relocated here in 1873, was in 1879 designated a fort. It was a headquarters in the campaigns of defense against and pursuit of the Apache chief Geronimo and lesser leaders, notably the Apache Kid. Because it was near a town, the fort was considered lighter duty than most such forts, and officers and their wives vied for assignment here during the Indian wars.

The site was especially pleasant, being at the confluence of the Pantano and Tanque Verde creeks, which joined to form the Rillito Creek, making an oasis in the desert country. Adobe and wood were the building materials of the fort. Most of the buildings lie in ruins today, but the reconstruction of the commanding officer's house provides a glimpse of the larger picture. The interior is furnished as officers' quarters might have been, with a mix of types of furnishings that might have made the trip west.

Geronimo's surrender to the United States Army in 1886 marked the beginning of the fort's decline. It was closed down in 1891. By the 1920s the site, then in great disrepair and partially abandoned to the elements, was increasingly seen as a historic place worthy of preservation. First it became a recreational park, with the ruins preserved. Limited reconstruction began in the 1960s with the commanding officer's house.

McALLISTER HOUSE 1873

Colorado Springs, Colorado

Major Henry McAllister, a native of Wilmington, Delaware, built this villa two years after the town of Colorado Springs was established. In the high, dry country, at the foot of Pike's Peak, McAllister created a residence that would have been fashionable anywhere in the country at the time and here was stylish indeed. The architect was George Summers, a Philadelphian who had come west from a world where the Queen Anne and Gothic modes were just becoming fashionable. He had taken a job with the Colorado Springs Company, a development enterprise in which McAllister was a director. Summers' house for McAllister shows a sure grasp of the sort of design Calvert Vaux had popularized in the post-Civil War period. Made to appear quaint and capenter-made, such houses glorified the simple life of the cottager and evoked an innocent past. At the same time the McAllister House has a fortress-like feeling; as its walls were rising a storm caused such damage that McAllister ordered all its dimensions thickened.

The picturesque villa, set behind a picket fence and enveloped in gardens, was well established by 1876, when the Colorado territory was granted statehood. Throngs of Indians and pioneer wagon trains passed its gate, sometimes stopping for water, and now and then to spend the night in the protection of the yard. The McAllister family lived in the house for eighty-seven years. Today it is furnished to represent late nineteenth-century life in Colorado.

HOTEL DE PARIS MUSEUM 1875

Georgetown, Colorado

Louis Dupuy, who founded the Hotel de Paris and operated it until his death in 1900, was born in Alençon, in France, as Adolphe François Gérard, the son of an innkeeper. He was reared to be a priest, but at the age of twenty he left the monastery. He went to Paris, found work in a hotel, and learned his first lessons in French cookery. He moved to London, then to New York, where he joined the army. Military service proved even less congenial than the priesthood, so he deserted, fled to Colorado, and changed his name to Louis Dupuy. A short career as a miner left him in bed convalescing from injury in an explosion and convinced that "in this land of gold and silver, we should live like princes. We should have a great hostelry and the best of wines."

In Georgetown, a civilized little city of 5,000, he called on public subscription to help him found a hotel. He gave himself completely to the project, remodeling an existing building into one of the best known hotels in the west. The finest foods and wines were imported to his establishment, and his flair for decor made his accommodations ever more glamorous. Art works of all kinds were acquired for the hotel. Walnut and silver maple flooring in the dining room was brought from the Great Lakes region. Furniture in the bedrooms was luxurious, buttoned and fringed; eventually there were bathrooms with porcelain lavatories and waterclosets. The hotel has come down intact, touched only by the hand of the conservationist. It evokes magnificently the gold and silver days it once knew—like the movies, but real.

MANDEL POST OFFICE 1878

Sheridan, Wyoming

This log house of twelve by fifteen feet was built by Phil Mandel in 1878. Mandel opened a store here and usurped the agency to receive and transmit mail. The arrangement was informal: Mail was deposited in a tin cracker box beside the door, and those seeking their mail shuffled through it from time to time to see if letters awaited them. After four years Mandel sold his cabin and property to John D. Loucks for $50. The single room, with a kitchen added to the side, served him and his family as a home. Taking his cue from Mandel, Loucks applied for and won the designation as postmaster, which brought a salary of $53.80 per year. He made his home the center of the town. Wyoming's first school was held in the kitchen, and its first church met in the main cabin Mandel had built. The post office was selected as the site for the territory's first election. In 1885 Loucks sold the cabin for use as its first bank.

Many a marble pile can claim less history that this small cabin. When a new brick bank was built, the cabin was rolled to the back of the property, then covered with clapboards on the outside, tin-roofed, and plastered within. The building was rented as offices, as a house, and even once as a ballet studio. At one point it was to be demolished, but when the logs appeared behind some siding, it was clear that the building was too historic to raze. The Wyoming Society moved the cabin to safer ground, and in 1976 it was restored to celebrate the national bicentennial. The roof was covered again in prairie sod, as it had been, and maintenance includes watering and cutting the wild grass.

OVERHOLSER MANSION 1902

Oklahoma City, Oklahoma

Henry and Anna Overholser employed the Kansas City architect W. S. Matthews to design their house, which was begun in 1902 on land purchased by Mrs. Overholser in the same year. It was to be a mansion in the French "chateauesque" style, built of Texas limestone, local sandstone, and brick, the main house of some 11,000 square feet, with an adjacent stable of 4,000 square feet. Overholser ordered that it be fully modern, with central heating, electric light and gas, and state-of-the art plumbing. Kansas City was a great style setter in this region and down through Texas to the Gulf Coast. The booming metropolis supported a large contingent of architecture offices and decorating establishments that built and outfitted mansions such as this in great numbers for cattle and oil entrepreneurs.

The Overholser house is a classic example of the big-house mode of the turn of the century throughout the country, but with a special character one associates with its region. Its ample rooms have broad windows, high ceilings, and great interior openings that make large suites for entertaining or comfortable summertime circulation. Massive woodwork, from the door finish to the staircase, is both natural, in polished oak, and painted; the plaster walls are covered with canvas, which is painted with fancy decorations. There are fifteen rooms, and in each of them one feels encased in sturdy structure. The house remained in the family until purchased for use as a house museum in 1980. The interiors are left as last used by the Overholsers.

THE PACIFIC WEST

In the area that is now California, Spanish settlement flourished in the third quarter of the eighteenth century. Anglo-Americans came to California as early as the 1820s with the arrival of Yankee seamen, but this group of pioneers did not settle permanently in Oregon until about 1840, and then under conditions of hardship not faced farther south on the Pacific coast. Hawaii had a different story, being the only former domain of a crowned king in residence to become an American state. The range of architectural examples is very great, and for the early years the most notable of these are in the vernacular, imported from Mexico and the eastern states of the Union. The adobe of the Indians and early Latin settlers found adaptation in many forms of building. Houses of milled lumber, such as the Octagon House in San Francisco, enjoyed prestige among the Anglo-American settlers, as did brick, stone, and even experimental cements and masticks, as at Honolulu's 'Iolani Palace, with the Victorians. The nineteenth-century buildings show the influence of climate on architecture in its relationship to the outdoors, a characteristic that would shape some of the region's most distinctive architecture in the twentieth century.

LA CASA DE ESTUDILLO 1829

San Diego, California

This house is one of the few examples of the hacienda form remaining in the United States. Many of these houses still exist in Mexico, some in ruins, others in use today. This one was built by José Antonio Estudillo and Maria Victoria Dominguez. Estudillo's father had been commander of the San Diego Presidio, one of a chain of forts the Spanish had built along the Pacific as far north as San Francisco. Independent Mexico began a program of secularizing church land holdings, and officials usually profited. This was the case for the entire Estudillo family, which came to own many thousands of acres.

When this house was dedicated in 1829, Estudillo was twenty-four and his wife was younger. Time would see the hacienda develop into a large, U-shaped building, with a shady central patio and rooms opening into rooms. A floor plan made in 1856 shows that, although some of the interior partitions have changed, the house is almost the same today as it was then. For the rest of their lives José Antonio and Maria Victoria lived here, reared their children, and entertained with warm hospitality.

The family stayed on until 1887, when a son, Salvador, moved out and left the house with a caretaker who stripped it and sold the materials for his own profit. The house was sold in 1909 to John D. Spreckles, who had it restored. By that time it was famous as a setting of Helen Hunt Jackson's popular novel *Ramona* (1884) and had spun a web of romance all its own. Acquired by the state, it was restored again in 1968. Today it is the centerpiece of Old Town San Diego.

OCTAGON HOUSE 1861

San Francisco, California

San Francisco's phenomenal growth during the Gold Rush left many examples of good architecture from the 1850s and later. Among the smaller and more choice examples is the Octagon House. This was an experimental house—indeed, a philosophical house—early in a strain that was to continue into our own time. Its inspiration came from a book by Orson Fowler, *The Octagon: Or A Home for All*, first published in 1847 and in many editions thereafter. This book, which promoted practical, comfortable living in an octagon-shaped house, led to a mania for such dwellings.

Although the interiors of the Octagon House have been changed and furnished in objects some thirty to fifty years earlier than the building, the house holds tenaciously to its Victorian character. Externally, where it is truly restored, it looks a bit like a pepper mill or a faceted ginger jar. The octagon shape is emphasized by the wooden quoins at the corners, and the structure is surmounted by a lantern that peaks the roof and once provided wonderful views of the harbor. Within, the rooms were originally more or less pie-shaped, around a central hall with a stairwell which, with the lantern, helped ventilation by creating a chimney-like draw of air from the rooms.

The builder, William C. McElroy, stashed away what was apparently a cornerstone box or time capsule, discovered during restoration in 1953. In the tin container, with a daguerreotype of himself with his wife Harriet, their daughter, and a nephew, he put a letter describing life then in San Francisco. "Look whichever way you will," he wrote, "and you observe happiness, prosperity and wealth."

MOUNT PLEASANT HOUSE 1876

Los Angeles, California

When William Hayes Perry arrived in California in 1853 hoping to strike it rich, he was worn out, ragged, and penniless from the arduous overland journey. He bought two suits on credit and set himself up as a carpenter. He soon graduated to investments in logging, and within a decade a lumber mill made him a rich man. By the late 1860s he was profitably engaged in a gas company and banking, as well as lumber. Meanwhile, in 1858, he married Elizabeth Dalton, who had traveled with her family to California from the east.

His house, built in 1876, is an Italianate mansion of wood, designed with great richness and style. An early drawing shows it in a deep garden, with cedars of Lebanon along the front walk and picket fencing with urns mounted on the posts.

An ornate porch wraps around two sides, and cresting crowns this and the roof. Inside, freestanding Corinthian columns form a screen in the double parlors; and elsewhere are ample rooms, flooded with light, elegant in black walnut and bird's-eye maple. The Perrys shipped most of their new furniture from the East, much of it in the currently popular French styles, as well as the more fashionable Queen Anne.

The Perrys lived here for only two years and sold the house to Judge Stephen C. Hubbell, president and founder of two railroad companies and a founder of the University of Southern California. After many years the house fell into disrepair and stood in the way of new development. Just before Christmas 1975 it was moved to Heritage Square, a park created to receive just such threatened buildings as this. It has been restored to the period of its building.

HOOVER-MINTHORN HOUSE MUSEUM 1881

Newberg, Oregon

This plain frame house, with its deep eaves, was from 1884 to 1889 the boyhood home of Herbert Hoover. Built in 1881 by Jesse Edwards, the founder of the town of Newberg, the house was purchased in 1884 by Henry John Minthorn, a physician who had come to Newberg as superintendent of a Quaker school, Friends Pacific Academy. He, his wife Laura, three daughters, and a son moved here in 1884. After the son died in an accident, Dr. and Mrs. Minthorn longed for another boy. It happened that Dr. Minthorn's sister Hulda, a widow, had died at West Branch, Iowa, leaving a young family. The Minthorns invited Herbert Hoover, age ten—called "Bert"—to come and live with them.

When he arrived it was summer, and there was a full crop of fruit in the orchards around the house. The family was making pear butter in the yard. Hoover, who had never tasted a pear, was told he could have all he wanted, which he willingly took, and went to bed sick. Every other memory of the place was happy for him. When in 1889 the Minthorns decided to move to Salem, he entered Stanford University. In 1955, at the age of 81, the former president attended the dedication of the house as a museum and recalled his life there in the 1880s.

Diligent effort has brought back many of the original furnishings to the house. All the furniture in Herbert Hoover's bedroom is original, and some items elsewhere in the house belong to the Minthorns and people they knew. Beyond its associations as a presidential site, the Hoover-Minthorn House provides an intimate picture of domestic life in the Willamette Valley in the late nineteenth century.

'IOLANI PALACE 1883

Honolulu, Hawaii

Iolani Palace was occupied by the last king and his sister, the last queen, of Hawaii, from 1883 until the fall of the kingdom in 1893. It was built by King David Kalakaua, from designs by the Australian Thomas Rowe, as revised in 1880 by Charles J. Wall of San Francisco. Inside, a grand stair is central to the great hall, flanked by a dining room and drawing room, both heroic in scale, and a crimson and gold throne room with motifs of palm fronds and spears.

The house is not especially Hawaiian. Traditionally the kings had lived very simply in large and informal houses, the simplest built of palm branches (sometimes hung with glass chandeliers inside) and the most complicated built of lumber, rather like Gulf Coast cottages, responding entirely to the climate. Even as the walls of the palace were rising, King Kalakaua moved into a comfortable rose-pink bungalow on the grounds, where he was visited by his many friends, including Mark Twain and Robert Louis Stevenson.

By the time the palace was built the Hawaiian monarchy had come under the control and influence of American sugar interests and other business groups that needed not only the ports Hawaii offered, but also the rich fields and cheap labor. Gaslit, plumbed, carpeted, and draped, the palace symbolized in a way the inevitable fall of the crown it was built to house. After hard use as a state capitol from 1893 until 1969 a notable restoration has returned large numbers of original objects, including the royal crowns.

HISTORIC PROPERTIES OWNED OR SUPPORTED BY THE NATIONAL SOCIETY OF THE COLONIAL DAMES OF AMERICA

Properties listed here without *annotation are owned (building and land) by the respective Colonial Dames state society. Annotations indicate other ownership; occupancy under a lease or other agreement; or other involvement such as contribution of financial or volunteer support or donation of furnishings or other objects.*

Properties marked with an asterisk (*) are listed on the National Register of Historic Places. Properties marked with a double asterisk (**) have a National Historic Landmark designation.

ALABAMA

CONDÉ-CHARLOTTE MUSEUM HOUSE* 1822
104 Theatre Street
Mobile

ARIZONA

JOHN C. FRÉMONT HOUSE MUSEUM* circa 1860
(La Casa del Gobernador)
151 South Granada Avenue
Tucson
The house is owned by the state of Arizona and administered by the Arizona Historical Society. The dining room is dedicated to NSCDA-Arizona.

FORT LOWELL MUSEUM* 1873; 1963
2900 North Craycroft Road
Tucson
The museum is a branch of the Arizona Historical Society. NSCDA-Arizona has contributed furnishings and financial support.

ARKANSAS

BROWNLEE-NOLAND HOUSE 1840s
The Arkansas Territorial Restoration
214 East Third Street
Little Rock
The house is part of the Arkansas Territorial Restoration, which is owned by the state of Arkansas and administered by the Department of Arkansas Heritage. NSCDA has contributed furnishings and financial support.

CALIFORNIA

LA CASA DE ESTUDILLO** 1829
Old Town, San Diego State Historical Park
San Diego
The house is owned and maintained by the state of California. NSCDA-California furnished the house and restored the garden.

OCTAGON HOUSE* 1861
2645 Gough Street
San Francisco

MOUNT PLEASANT HOUSE* 1876
(Heritage Square)
3800 Homer Street
Los Angeles
NSCDA-California owns and manages the house. The land is owned by the City of Los Angeles Department of Recreation and Parks and managed by Heritage Square/Cultural Heritage Foundation of Los Angeles.

COLORADO

McALLISTER HOUSE* 1874
423 North Cascade Avenue
Colorado Springs

HOTEL DE PARIS MUSEUM* 1875
409 Sixth Street
Georgetown

CONNECTICUT

WEBB-DEANE-STEVENS MUSEUM
203-215 Main Street
Wethersfield
Joseph Webb House** 1752
Silas Deane House** 1766
Isaac Stevens House* 1788

DELAWARE

FIRST PRESBYTERIAN CHURCH* 1740
1740 West Street and Park Drive
Wilmington
NSCDA-Delaware owns and maintains the building. The land is owned by New Castle County and maintained by the Parks and Recreation Department.

First Presbyterian Church

DISTRICT OF COLUMBIA

DUMBARTON HOUSE
(NSCDA NATIONAL HEADQUARTERS)* 1799
2715 Q Street, N.W.

FLORIDA

XIMENEZ-FATIO HOUSE* 1798
20 Aviles Street
St. Augustine

CLARA BARKLEY DORR HOUSE* 1871
311 South Adams Street
Pensacola
The house is owned by the Historic Pensacola Preservation Board, an agency of the Florida Department of State. The Pensacola Town Committee, NSCDA-Florida, provides furnishings, docents, and volunteer assistance.

GEORGIA

ANDREW LOW HOUSE 1848
329 Abercorn Street
Savannah

HARDAWAY HOUSE 1856
522 North Dawson Street
Thomasville

Hardaway House

RANKIN HOUSE* 1850-1870
1440 Second Avenue
Columbus
The house is owned by Historic Columbus Foundation. The Columbus Town Committee, NSCDA-Georgia, assisted with restoration, contributed furnishings, and maintains two of the rooms.

FOUNDERS' EXHIBIT*
Okefenokee Heritage Center, Inc.
North Augusta Avenue
Waycross
The Waycross Town Committee, NSCDA-Georgia, contributed furnishings and assists with staffing.

Founders' Exhibit

HAWAII

'IOLANI PALACE** 1883
King and Richard Streets
Honolulu
The palace is owned and operated by the state of Hawaii. NSCDA-Hawaii gives financial support to Friends of 'Iolani Palace restoration funds.

ILLINOIS

CLARKE HOUSE MUSEUM* 1836
1800 South Prairie Avenue
Chicago
The property is owned and maintained by the city of Chicago. The house is operated jointly by the city, NSCDA-Illinois, and the Chicago Architecture Foundation. NSCDA-Illinois provides furnishings and financial support for their maintenance.

INDIANA

DAVID LENTZ HOUSE* 1820
Historic New Harmony
Intersection of Indiana routes 66 and 68,
seven miles south of Interstate 64
The house is owned by NSCDA-Indiana and leased to Historic New Harmony, a division of the University of Southern Indiana.

J. F. D. LANIER STATE HISTORIC SITE* 1844
511 West First Street
Madison
NSCDA-Indiana assists the Indiana Department of Natural Resources in the restoration and refurbishing of the house, a part of the Indiana State Museum System.

EIGHTEENTH-CENTURY ROOM, EMPIRE ROOM
Lilly Pavilion of Decorative Arts
Indianapolis Museum of Art
Indianapolis
Rooms are sponsored by NSCDA-Indiana.

Eighteenth-Century Room, Empire Room

IOWA

PLUM GROVE* 1845
1030 Carroll Street
Iowa City
The house is owned and maintained by the Iowa Department of Natural Resources. NSCDA-Iowa furnishes, decorates, and supervises the house.

CODY-MCCAUSLAND HOUSE* 1847, 1870
Route 61 North
Davenport
The property is owned and administered by the Scott County Conservation Board. NSCDA-Iowa has contributed furnishings.

FLYNN MANSION* 1870
Living History Farms
2600 111th Street, Urbandale (Route 1)
Des Moines
The house is owned by Living History Farms Foundation. NSCDA-Iowa has contributed furnishings and other household items.

KENTUCKY

LIBERTY HALL** 1796
218 Wilkinson Street
Frankfort

ORLANDO BROWN HOUSE* 1835
202 Wilkinson Street
Frankfort

LOUISIANA

KENT PLANTATION HOUSE* 1796
3601 Bayou Rapides Road
Alexandria
The house is owned and managed by Kisatchie Delta Regional Planning and Development District, Inc. The land is owned by the American Legion. NSCDA-Louisiana has contributed furnishings and gives financial support.

HERMANN-GRIMA HISTORIC HOUSE** 1831
820 St. Louis Street
New Orleans
The house is owned by the Christian Women's Exchange. NSCDA-Louisiana has contributed furnishings.

ISAIAH GARRETT LAW OFFICE MUSEUM* 1840
520 South Grand Street
Monroe
The property is owned by the city of Monroe, which leases it to the Monroe Committee, NSCDA-Louisiana. The committee has restored the house and provides upkeep and tours.

Isaiah Garrett Law Office Museum

OAKLEY PLANTATION HOUSE* 1799
Audubon Memorial Park
West Feliciana Parish (St. Francisville)
The house is owned by the state of Louisiana. NSCDA-Louisiana contributed furnishings. The Baton Rouge and River Parishes Committee gives financial support.

SPRING STREET MUSEUM* 1866
525 Spring Street
Shreveport

Spring Street Museum

HEADQUARTERS HOUSE 1871
1413 Louisiana Avenue
New Orleans

Headquarters House

MAINE

TATE HOUSE** 1755
1270 Westbrook Street
Portland

MARYLAND

MOUNT CLARE MUSEUM HOUSE** 1760
Carroll Park
1500 Washington Boulevard
Baltimore
NSCDA-Maryland owns the furnishings, maintains the interior, and operates the house as a museum under contract with the city of Baltimore. The surrounding park is maintained by the Bureau of Parks and Recreation.

MASSACHUSETTS

MARTIN HOUSE* 1728
North Swansea

QUINCY HOMESTEAD* 1706; renovated 1904
1010 Hancock Street
Quincy
NSCDA-Massachusetts acquired the house in 1904, renovated it, then donated it to the Metropolitan District Commission, which maintains it and the grounds. NSCDA-Massachusetts furnished the house, operates it, and conducts tours.

WILLIAM HICKLING PRESCOTT HOUSE** 1808
55 Beacon Street
Boston

MICHIGAN

COMMANDER'S RESIDENCE* 1880
Historic Fort Wayne
6325 West Jefferson
Detroit
The property is owned by the city of Detroit and administered by the Detroit Historical Museum. NSCDA-Michigan provided research, furnishings, and funding for the restoration of the interior to the period of the house.

MINNESOTA

ALEXANDER RAMSEY HOUSE*
1872
265 South Exchange Street
St. Paul
NSCDA-Minnesota is represented on the board of governors and oversees the running of the house along with the Minnesota Historical Society, which owns the property.

MISSISSIPPI

EVANSVIEW-BONTURA HOUSE* 1790
107 Broadway
Natchez

THE OAKS* 1853
823 North Jefferson Street
Jackson

MISSOURI

LOUIS BOLDUC HOUSE** 1775
123 South Main Street
Ste. Genevieve

LINDEN HOUSE* circa 1809
116 South Main Street
Ste. Genevieve

Linden House

THORNHILL GRANARY AND DISTILLERY* 1819
Faust Park
15185 Olive Boulevard
Chesterfield
The properties are owned by the St. Louis County Department of Parks and Recreation. NSCDA-Missouri contributed to the restoration and furnishings of the buildings.

Thornhill Granary and Distillery

BOLDUC–LE MEILLEUR HOUSE** circa 1820
121 South Main Street
Ste. Genevieve

Bolduc–Le Meilleur House

CAMPBELL HOUSE* 1851
1508 Locust Street
St. Louis
The house is owned and operated by the Campbell House Foundation. NSCDA-Missouri contributed furnishings and provides financial support.

JOHN WORNALL HOUSE* 1858
146 West 61st Terrace
Kansas City
The house is owned and operated by the Jackson County Historical Society. NSCDA-Missouri has contributed funds to restoration, furnishing, maintenance, programs, and the establishment of the garden.

NEW HAMPSHIRE

MOFFATT-LADD HOUSE** 1763
154 Market Street
Portsmouth

NEW JERSEY

PEACHFIELD PLANTATION HOUSE* 1725; 1931
Burrs Road
Mount Holly

THE OLD SCHOOL HOUSE* 1759
35 Brainerd Street
Mount Holly

The Old School House

NEW MEXICO

PALACE OF THE GOVERNORS* (EXHIBITION) 1610
The Plaza
Santa Fe
The Palace is owned by the state of New Mexico and administered by the Museum of New Mexico. Museum collection includes NSCDA-New Mexico's exhibition of artifacts from the Spanish Colonial period collected by the society.

NEW YORK

VAN CORTLANDT HOUSE MUSEUM** 1748
Van Cortlandt Park
Broadway at 246th Street
The Bronx
The house is owned by the city of New York. NSCDA-New York restored it and operates it under a licensing agreement with the city.

COLONIAL DAMES MUSEUM HOUSE (HEADQUARTERS) 1930
(NSCDA in New York Museum House)
215 East 71st Street
New York

NORTH CAROLINA

JOEL LANE HOUSE* 1760s
728 West Hargett Street
Raleigh

NSCDA-North Carolina leases the house and grounds to the Joel Lane House, Inc., a non-profit organization formed for the restoration, maintenance, and operation of the house.

BURGWIN-WRIGHT HOUSE* 1770
244 Market Street
Wilmington

OVAL BALLROOM* 1830
Adjacent to 225 Dick Street
Heritage Square
Fayetteville
The property is owned by the Women's Club of Fayetteville. The Cumberland County Committee, NSCDA-North Carolina, provided the furnishings.

HAYWOOD HALL HOUSE AND GARDENS* 1798
211 New Bern Avenue
Raleigh

FOURTH HOUSE 1767
Old Salem, Inc.
438 South Main Street
Winston-Salem
NSCDA-North Carolina leases the house to Old Salem, Inc.

Fourth House

HISTORIC ROSEDALE* circa 1805
3427 North Tryon Street
Charlotte
The house is owned by the Historic Rosedale Board, Inc. The Mecklenburg Committee, NSCDA-North Carolina, led the fundraising for its purchase and restoration, is represented on the board, and provides volunteers.

OHIO

CHARLESTON ROOM
Cincinnati Art Museum
Eden Park
Cincinnati
Museum room was furnished by NSCDA-Ohio.

KEMPER LOG HOUSE 1804
Sharon Woods Village
Sharonville
NSCDA-Ohio owns the house and furnishings. The land is owned by the city of Cincinnati as part of a city park. The house is managed by Historic Southwest Ohio under a contract with NSCDA-Ohio.

WOLCOTT HOUSE 1827
1031 River Road
Maumee
The house is owned by the city of Maumee and leased to the Maumee Valley Historical Society. The Toledo Circle, NSCDA-Ohio, contributed funds to the restoration, furnishings, and artifacts and developed the original room of the house into the Wolcott History Room.

Wolcott House

OKLAHOMA

OVERHOLSER MANSION* 1902
Heritage Hill Historical Preservation District
405 N.W. 15th Street
Oklahoma City
The house is owned by the state of Oklahoma and administered by the Oklahoma Historical Society. NSCDA-Oklahoma has provided assistance in acquiring, cataloging, and preserving artifacts, has contributed to renovation, and is represented on the advisory board.

THOMAS GILCREASE HOUSE 1903
1400 N. Gilcrease Museum Road
Tulsa
The house is owned by the city of Tulsa and leased to the Tulsa Historical Society. NSCDA-Oklahoma has restored several rooms.

Thomas Gilcrease House

OREGON

MCLOUGHLIN HOUSE*
(DINING ROOM) 1846
713 Center Street
Oregon City
The house is maintained by the McLoughlin House Memorial Association and the grounds are maintained by the city. NSCDA-Oregon restored and furnished the dining room and provides docents.

McLoughlin House (Dining Room)

HOOVER-MINTHORN HOUSE MUSEUM* 1881
115 South River Street
Newberg

JEFFERSON ROOM
Oregon Historical Center
1234 S.W. Park Avenue
Portland
NSCDA-Oregon raised funds for the room and its furnishings.

Jefferson Room

PENNSYLVANIA

STENTON** 1723
18th Street and Windrim Avenue
Philadelphia
The house is owned by the city of Philadelphia and maintained by NSCDA-Pennsylvania.

WOODVILLE, THE JOHN NEVILLE HOUSE** 1789
Washington Pike (Pennsylvania Route 50)
Collier Township
The house is owned by the Pittsburgh History and Landmarks Foundation. The Allegheny County Committee, NSCDA-Pennsylvania, restored and furnished the dining room and provides docents.

COLONIAL DAMES HOUSE (HEADQUARTERS) 1921
1630 Latimer Street
Philadelphia

Colonial Dames House (Headquarters)

RHODE ISLAND

GOVERNOR STEPHEN HOPKINS HOUSE** 1707; 1742
10 Hopkins Street
Providence

The property is owned by the state of Rhode Island and held in custody by NSCDA-Rhode Island, which is responsible for maintenance of the interior of the house and of the gardens.

WHITEHALL HOUSE MUSEUM* 1729
Berkeley Avenue
Middletown

SOUTH CAROLINA

THE POWDER MAGAZINE** 1713
79 Cumberland Avenue
Charleston

The Powder Magazine

HANOVER HOUSE* 1714
Clemson University
Clemson
The house is owned by and is on the campus of Clemson University. It was furnished by the Spartanburg Committee, NSCDA-South Carolina.

TENNESSEE

TRAVELLERS REST HISTORIC HOUSE MUSEUM* 1799; 1828
636 Farrell Parkway
Nashville
NSCDA-Tennessee leases the property to Travellers Rest Historic House Museum, Inc., and is represented on the board.

TEXAS

NEILL-COCHRAN MUSEUM HOUSE* 1855
2310 San Gabriel Street
Austin

VERMONT

GENEALOGICAL LIBRARY
The Bennington Museum
West Main Street
Bennington
NSCDA-Vermont provided furnishings and has given financial support for purchase of books.

Genealogical Library

VIRGINIA

WILTON HOUSE MUSEUM**
1753; 1934
215 South Wilton Road
Richmond

GUNSTON HALL PLANTATION** 1755
Lorton
The property is owned by the commonwealth of Virginia and administered by a Board of Regents composed of representatives from each NSCDA state society.

WASHINGTON

EIGHTEENTH-CENTURY DRAWING ROOM
Museum of History and Industry
2700 Twenty-fourth Avenue East
Seattle
Museum room displays eighteenth-century furnishings and other objects collected by NSCDA-Washington, which funded design and construction of the room.

Eighteenth-Century Drawing Room

WEST VIRGINIA

CRAIK-PATTON HOUSE* 1834
2809 Kanawha Boulevard East
Charleston
NSCDA-West Virginia owns the house and leases the land from the city of Charleston.

WISCONSIN

INDIAN AGENCY HOUSE* 1832
Fort Winnebago
Highway 33
Portage

KILBOURNTOWN HOUSE* 1844
Estabrook Park
Milwaukee
The property is owned by Milwaukee County and administered by the Milwaukee County Historical Society and the Park Commission. NSCDA-Wisconsin owns the furnishings and is responsible for historical presentation.

WYOMING

MANDEL POST OFFICE 1878
Trails End Historical Center
400 Clarendon Street
Sheridan
NSCDA-Wyoming owns and maintains the house, which is located on the grounds of the state of Wyoming's Trails End Historical Center.

ENGLAND

SULGRAVE MANOR 1539
Sulgrave, near Banbury
Northamptonshire
The manor is owned by the people of the United States and Great Britain. NSCDA assisted in its restoration, endowed it in perpetuity, contributes to its upkeep, and is represented on the board that administers the property.

Sulgrave Manor